T0305000

THE QUIZMASTER

THE QUIZMASTER

JAY FLYNN

WITH
GARRY JENKINS

**HODDER &
STOUGHTON**

First published in Great Britain in 2024 by Hodder & Stoughton Limited
An Hachette UK company

2

A CIP catalogue record for this title is available from the British Library

Hardback ISBN 9781399722483
ebook ISBN 9781399722490

Typeset in Plantin Light by Hewer Text UK Ltd, Edinburgh
Printed and bound in Great Britain by Clays Ltd, Elcograf S.p.A.

Hodder & Stoughton policy is to use papers that are natural, renewable
and recyclable products and made from wood grown in sustainable
forests. The logging and manufacturing processes are expected to
conform to the environmental regulations of the country of origin.

Hodder & Stoughton Limited
Carmelite House
50 Victoria Embankment
London EC4Y 0DZ

www.hodder.co.uk

To Jack

Sometimes, all you need to do is ask the questions.

Prologue

THE BENCH

Who said: Knowing yourself is the beginning of all wisdom?
Jay's Virtual Pub Quiz No 13, April 2020

I was compiling a quiz a few years ago when I came across a saying that really struck me: *We each lead two lives. The one we learn with and the one we live after that.*

It hit a nerve, mainly because it sounded so wise and truthful, but also because I got the feeling that, maybe, it applied to me.

I filed it away with all the other random information that's stored in my brain, then forgot about it. I hadn't expected it to pop up again. But then, one day in December 2021, it did. It was the day my two lives collided. The day I realised those words definitely applied to me.

I had made a trip to London for an event on the Victoria Embankment, overlooking the Thames. It was a crisp, clear morning and the riverside looked its picture-postcard best. The sky was a flawless blue. The golds and silvers of Big Ben, the London Eye, St Paul's and the Shard glimmered and glinted in the wintry sun. The grey-green waters of the Thames were alive with working boats and dredgers, their backwash slapping noisily against the river wall.

I hadn't been back for a while, but I knew this corner of the city well. Being here quickly stirred up old memories and emotions. They were mixed up with a more immediate, uneasy feeling. And a question that was whirring around in my head: *Why am I here?*

I'd been asked to unveil a plaque on one of the benches that line this stretch of the riverfront. I was also due to give a little speech to thank the fundraisers and supporters who had come up with the idea for the brass memorial. On the rail journey down to London from my adopted home in Darwen, Lancashire, all sorts of other questions had been swirling around. They were coming so fast, at times I felt like they were outrunning the train. That wasn't unusual for me. I have an overactive brain. I tend to overthink things. Overdramatise, often.

My first concern was whether I should even have made the trip. There were still COVID restrictions in place and, with the spread of the new Omicron strain, there was talk of a new national lockdown in the UK around Christmas. Who'd risk travelling here to central London just for this? Wasn't it endangering people's health? And what about my wife and young son back home, was I putting them at risk?

Subconsciously, I suspect I was preparing myself. Protecting myself, too. I didn't really expect many people to turn up. Who was going to attend a ceremony where I was the guest of honour? My imposter syndrome was on steroids.

I should have been used to it – my life had been like this for a while. Ever since the private little online quiz night I'd started for my friends in Darwen at the beginning of the UK's first coronavirus lockdown in 2020 had turned into something beyond even my wildest imagination. But I'd never quite got my head around it. Hundreds of thousands of people had taken part in my quizzes each week. Somehow, I had transformed from an ordinary guy struggling to put food on the table for his family into, well . . . I didn't even like using the word . . . a celebrity. One who unveiled plaques. How had I managed to connect with so many where others hadn't?

Fortunately, I arrived at the riverside bench to see that the small crowd that had gathered contained some friendly and familiar faces. They immediately put me at ease. I made my speech, performed the unveiling, then posed for photographs and spoke to the handful of journalists who had turned up. It was a lovely occasion. I felt proud to have been part of it. To have supported the charities and the people involved. As the ceremony drew to a close and everyone drifted away, I hung back. I wanted to spend a moment sitting on the bench, decompressing, taking stock.

There was a good reason I'd been invited to the occasion. It was why I'd agreed to travel down to attend but also why I'd been most anxious about coming back here to the Embankment. I knew I'd have to confront my past.

A decade earlier, I'd been homeless. For two years, I'd spent my days wandering the streets of London and my nights sleeping rough. This bench had been my home for most of that time. I'd slept here almost every night. So it was no surprise that the memories began to flood back. The good and the bad, mostly the bad.

I'd spent long, lonely, vulnerable nights on this bench, wrapped up in a sleeping bag, barely a penny to my name, a million thoughts exploding in my head, many of them of the darkest kind imaginable. I'd endured all weathers, watched the river rise and fall in all seasons. I'd felt my own emotions ebb and flow, dramatically at times. At my lowest, my mental health had been so fragile that I'd tried to end it all. And not just once.

Looking out on to the river today, I shook my head quietly. Had all that really happened to me? In all honesty, I wasn't sure how I'd survived.

All I knew was that I *had* made it. And with the help of some remarkable people – some of whom had been with me at the unveiling today – I'd rebuilt myself. I'd learned an awful lot about myself during that rehabilitation process. I'd begun to understand a fair bit about other people too. What connects and drives us. What we all need to survive. That knowledge had allowed me to re-enter society. As a stronger, better person. More capable of handling all that life threw at me.

A lot of water had flowed down the river past Waterloo Bridge and beyond since that desperate period. Not just for me. For everyone. The world had turned.

A lone tourist river cruiser was ploughing its way down the Thames. Not so long ago there would have been a flotilla of them, filled with visitors from around the globe on Christmas shopping breaks to London. A year and a half since the coronavirus outbreak, the vessel's decks were all but deserted. I glimpsed a few brave souls standing well apart, wearing face masks, taking in the iconic views. How different our world had become. We'd become. We'd all adapted and changed, learned new ways of living that we'd never have imagined. We'd had plenty of time to reflect, all of us. I suspected the pandemic would shape people for the rest of their lives.

It was then that it popped back into my head. That saying.

We each lead two lives. The one we learn with and the one we live after that.

I was much more open about it these days, but for a long time I'd been ashamed of my experience on the streets. I'd wished it away, denied it had even happened. It had been my dark secret. I had told very few people about my struggles and my homelessness. Why would I? What good would it do me? And what would people think of me once they knew? For a decade or so, I had basically persuaded myself it had happened to someone else. Another me, someone unconnected to the person I was today. I'd put it in a box and hidden it away.

Of course, I saw now that I'd been kidding myself.

The truth was, it *had* happened to me. My past had never gone away. But neither had the lessons I'd learned. They were a part of me too. We're all shaped and moulded by our experiences. The lives with which we learn. I was no different.

It was as if a light switch had been tripped. I began to see how important those lessons had been during these last, tumultuous, life-changing eighteen months. In truth, they'd been central to everything that had happened to me. The more I thought about it, the more sense it made. It explained so much. Answered so many of the questions I'd been wrestling with since my life had been upended the previous year. How had I connected with so many people? Why me? What had driven me to make certain choices along the way?

For a moment or two, I scolded myself. How had it taken me so long to see the wood for the trees? Why hadn't I seen how my first life had shaped and influenced my second? But then I laughed and shook my head again. My mind scrolled back to that time. To the beginning of the pandemic. And the uncertainty, fear and near panic that almost everyone had felt. How could I have been expected to see anything clearly in the midst of all that? It would have been impossible. Back then, in the early weeks of 2020, I had been like everyone else. I hadn't been giving the past much thought at all. I'd been too busy worrying about whether I had a future . . .

ROUND ONE

1

CLOSING TIME

Which motor company was previously known
as Swallow Sidecar Company?
Quiz 12, Jay's Virtual Pub Quiz Book 2

Karaoke is a Japanese word that translates to what in English?
Quiz 10, Jay's Virtual Pub Quiz Book 2

Who led the non-violent campaign for India's independence?
Jay's Virtual Pub Quiz No 10, March 2020

Looking back on it, I suppose I should laugh at the irony. At the beginning of 2020, the whole world was asking questions. Lots of them. Even though no one had any clear answers.

I, on the other hand, was completely obsessed with just one question. I couldn't get beyond it. It was dominating my life. It boiled down to a life-changing choice. Whether to cling on to my struggling business or to accept defeat and kiss goodbye to a dream?

The answer was staring me in the face.

★

Mahatma Gandhi once visited my adopted home of Darwen. He was given a tour of one of the town's textile factories in 1931, as part of his visit to the UK during his campaign for Indian independence.

Darwen is set in a picturesque river valley on the edge of the West Pennine Moors, twenty miles north-west of Manchester. During the Industrial Revolution of the mid-nineteenth century, the town was an industrial powerhouse, a centre for textile manufacturing. Samuel Crompton, the pioneering inventor of the spinning jenny, lived in the town for a while. But by the time of Gandhi's visit – ironically, in part because of his government's boycott of British cotton goods – the industry and its biggest factory, India Mill, had begun a slow decline.

Darwen was still a busy place, with a large paint factory and other successful businesses, but by January 2020 the boarded-up premises and streets lined with charity shops told their own story. It was another post-industrial northern town continuing the slow slide from its glory days. My own fading fortunes were tied up in another throwback to Darwen's once prosperous past – a pub, The Crown, a short walk from my home.

I'd taken over the premises as landlord the previous year. It had been a huge moment for me. I'd always been something of a Walter Mitty. A daydreamer. I'd fantasised about being a footballer, a Formula One racing driver, a singer. They were never going to happen. My dream of running my own pub had been far more realistic. And I'd achieved it. The thought of losing it so soon was breaking my heart.

★

I moved up to Lancashire from London in 2010, when I was in my late twenties. I'd followed my heart to live with a girlfriend in Wigan and liked it there. The relationship didn't last but my love of the area did. The old cliché about this corner of the north of England being one of the friendliest parts of the country was true.

It was meeting my wife, Sarah, in 2013 that drew me to Darwen. We had our first date in Bolton and hit it off immediately. We spent the entire night chatting and laughing together, and have been inseparable ever since. Opposites attract, they say, and in many ways we are very different characters. She's laid back and unflustered by life, whereas I can analyse and fret about everything to the nth degree. It's one of the reasons we work so well as a partnership, I suspect. We complement each other. Yin and yang. I can be something of an extrovert and enjoy my social life. I have never been one to sit in at night, I tend to get itchy feet. By contrast, Sarah is a real homely person, never happier than when she's watching TV or sharing a drink with friends or relatives. She's very close to her family, her mum, stepdad and three sisters. When I moved to Darwen, they welcomed me with open arms. In a way, Sarah gave me the family I hadn't had for a long time. In life, sometimes you don't realise what you want until you feel it. With Sarah, I knew I'd found something special, someone with whom I wanted to spend the rest of my life. We were married in 2016 and had our son, Jack, a year later.

Of course, my friends never missed an opportunity to remind me I was a Londoner. 'It's bath not baahth.' But I felt like I belonged, that my roots were here in Darwen and that I fitted in, which wasn't something I'd been able to say very often in my life.

Since 2014 I'd been working in the car industry, as a salesman and manager. As a bit of a 'petrol head' with an encyclopaedic knowledge of everything to do with cars and motor racing, it was a role that came fairly naturally to me. My sales philosophy was simple. Talk to people honestly. Leave out the BS. Focus on what they want. It had served me well, so far at least. I'd worked at a couple of big showrooms in the area selling Nissans, Peugeots and assorted other vehicles.

I've never been someone with a huge amount of confidence but working the forecourts and competing successfully with other salesmen and women gave me a new self-belief. A social life too. In Darwen, I forged real friendships.

With my car sales colleagues, I spent a fair bit of time in a local pub, The Greenfield, where Sarah ran the pub's weekly quiz. We had a team, naturally, made up mostly of colleagues and friends from the motor trade. I've always enjoyed quizzes. My mind has always been a store of useless information, so I have a knack for them.

For a brief time, I'd taken over from Sarah as the quizmaster. Even before Jack came along, she had found it increasingly hard to juggle the quiz with her job working locally as an administrator for the NHS. I spotted that she'd started putting together her quiz nights in a rush, lifting questions or sometimes entire quizzes from online sites. That was anathema to me. I offered to start compiling original quizzes, drawing on all sorts of sources from encyclopaedias to Wikipedia. I liked the process. Pulling together fifty or so random facts each week suited my overactive brain. Sarah had happily handed me the quizmaster's microphone. It didn't last long – a new landlord arrived and took it over for a time – but I enjoyed it while it lasted.

The Greenfield was a small pub, but it had a real atmosphere. I watched football there, celebrated New Year's Eve, took part in occasional, sometimes impromptu karaoke nights. But I knew from Sarah that the pub was headed on a downward slope. So, in September 2018, when Sarah's cousin Louise and her partner, Barry, who owned the premises, approached us about taking it over when the latest in a line of unsuccessful landlords left, I was in two minds, at first anyway. On the one hand, I'd always wanted to run a pub. On the other, I had a wife and a one-year-old son and plenty of debts I'd stacked up from the past. There was no way I could pay rent or anything like that. But they agreed to take care of the business side of things if I ran the pub on a day-to-day basis, drawing a salary as well.

I was told I'd be given a budget and free rein to do my own thing. The hope was that I'd be able to restore it to its former, thriving self.

The more I mulled over the offer, the more attractive it became. The economic outlook in the north of England wasn't great and selling cars had become tough. I'd begun to feel the pressure. It hadn't helped my mental health, something I'd learned I had to watch carefully. On top of this, a lot of the people with whom I'd enjoyed working had moved on, to be replaced by colleagues with whom I didn't get on so well. So, after a lot of agonising, I finally said yes. I applied for – and got – a licence to be a landlord. I was in business.

I knew that I'd need to come up with a few events and promotions to draw people back into The Greenfield. I introduced regular karaoke nights but also live music. I had local singers queuing up to do solo gigs on Saturday nights. It worked. People began to come back. I even got the local MP to come along and pose for photographs, which got us into the local newspaper. Things were soon going so well that Louise and Barry converted the upstairs into a restaurant.

I also took over the pub's weekly quiz again. It was all part of the job of being a pub landlord as far as I was concerned.

Despite this upturn in fortunes, I knew there wasn't much more room for expansion. It was a small pub. I'd probably taken it as far as I could. So when one of the bar staff, Paige, mentioned that another pub in the town was coming up for rent, my ears pricked up.

To be honest, I was surprised that The Crown was available. It was one of the oldest and best-established pubs in town, well known for its live music in particular. But I knew it had been closed for a few months. I was intrigued.

Paige and I arranged a discreet meeting with the area manager for the pub chain that owned The Crown. They provided us with some recent sales and profit figures and invited us to make a proposal. Paige said she could raise the money needed for the rent and the deposit and setting-up fees. It was a family loan, so I insisted that we would pay it back via the pub's profits from the get-go. I still wasn't in a position to put money in myself. What I did have, though, was a licence. I also did my bit by preparing a cash flow and business plan. I'm a numbers nerd, and I burned the midnight oil coming up with so many tables and projections you'd have thought I was launching a takeover of Tesco. My proposal was that we kept it as a music venue but introduced some new elements. Food was one option, but so too were more events like karaoke, bingo and quiz nights. To our mild amazement, the area manager went for it.

Fortunately, Louise and Barry weren't too disappointed at my departure. I'd turned the place around to such an extent they could run it themselves. The restaurant in particular was doing well for them. I was glad to part amicably.

We kept our plans for The Crown under wraps, which provided some fun. In a small town like Darwen, news spreads in minutes, so there was endless speculation about who had taken over. Someone mentioned a rumour that it was a Premier League footballer. Why a millionaire sportsman would take over a small-town pub was anyone's guess. Some of the theories were hilarious, others way off the mark. No one suspected us.

We got the keys on my thirty-seventh birthday, on Tuesday 9 April 2019. There was a small flat above the pub, which Paige moved into. It seemed only fair. She needed somewhere to live, and she'd raised the capital we needed. It also meant there was someone on the premises around the clock.

Our first job was to clear the place up. It was no small task – the pub was filthy inside, thick with dust and in need of deep, industrial-scale cleaning. It was all hands on deck, with friends and family joining Sarah, Paige and me in donning their rubber gloves. It was a tall order. We had ten days until we opened the following Friday night.

We managed it. I booked a singer I'd got to know from The Greenfield, set up a couple of free drink promotions and opened our doors. The novelty factor drew a few people in and one or two of the pub's old regulars reappeared. Business wasn't spectacular, but it was steady. For a short while at least, I felt we had a sporting chance of making it a success.

In many ways, running a pub is no different to running an airline or a restaurant, a fashion brand or a hotel. The key lies in generating some kind of loyalty. Getting a group of regulars that come in and spend money. I knew if I got that right, the pub would look after itself.

So I set to work in the late spring and summer of 2019, trying to do just that.

It saddens me that so many community pubs are closing across the country. As I knew myself, they are not just places to go and have a pint or a glass of wine or a gin and tonic. They are social centres, well-being hubs. People need them. So I was always attentive to our customers, as was Paige. Like me, she had a complicated family history and was attuned to people's frailties. Some people, of course, liked to just come in and sit in the corner, doing a crossword or reading the racing pages in the newspaper over a quiet pint. I left them to it. But for those who were looking for a convivial, open and friendly place to while away an hour or two, I was a visible and friendly landlord.

It seemed to pay off. As our customer base grew, we even became something of a refuge for local waifs and strays. One regular, a youngish lad who worked for the supermarket across the road, was painfully shy and anxious around other people. I befriended him and put him at ease. Slowly but surely, he found his feet and began to come out of himself. And a lady from Blackburn used to travel to The Crown just to take part in our Friday night karaoke session. She was a good singer and enjoyed herself. She always came on her own, but we kept an eye on her. On more than one occasion, we stepped in when she was receiving unwanted attention. I loved the idea that we were a safe haven. We even had a couple of lost souls who struck up a romance that eventually led to marriage. It fitted into my philosophy of wanting to build a real community. We'd soon grown close enough to some of our regulars that I'd occasionally give them a lift home at the end of the night.

The honeymoon period lasted a few months; it wasn't long before we ran into some headwinds.

The previous landlords still lived in the town, and I bumped into them a few weeks after taking over. They asked how I was getting on and wished me luck. The implication was that I'd need it. The figures we'd been given by the area manager had shown the pub had been through its peaks and troughs. I'd hoped I could arrest the downward curve of recent years, but it was proving harder than I had anticipated.

It wasn't hard for me to work out why we were struggling.

The Crown had been closed for four months. That's a long time for a pub to be out of the game. A new pub – a Wetherspoons, which specialised in selling cheap drinks and was also nearer the centre of town – had taken away a lot of the regulars. Added to this, the old Facebook page for the pub had been deleted. It had been quite popular, with a few thousand followers. I'd had to start from scratch with a new page. Building its following was tough. Every new follower and 'like' was hard won.

I'd also been frustrated by red tape and regulations at the pub. I'd had an idea to use a large, airy room upstairs for food or private functions, but that had been quickly scuppered. There was no fire escape so – according to health and safety rules – the most people we could have in there at any one time was six. That wasn't going to work at all.

Last but not least, when it came to the drinks we could stock, our hands were tied, quite literally. We were 'tied' to the company and had to buy all our stock through them. That limited the range of drinks we could sell, but more importantly it meant we couldn't buy alternative – cheaper – drinks, beers in particular. It was my first proper attempt at running a pub single-handed and the learning curve was steep. Still, we persevered. We put everything we had into it. And as things settled down, a pattern began to emerge. Our weekends were fairly busy, but it was Thursday nights that became our biggest money-spinner of the week. Thursday night was quiz night.

★

I read a quote somewhere a while back that there are two reasons British people love a pub quiz. We love a drink. And we love to be right.

That may or may not be true, but what's in no doubt is the fact that hundreds of thousands of people compete in pub quizzes each week. And if we're not in the pub pitting ourselves against each other, we're watching TV quizzes like *The Chase* and *Pointless*, *Mastermind* and *Who Wants to Be a Millionaire?* Famous quiz catch-phrases – 'I've started so I'll finish', 'We don't want to give you that', 'Here's your starter for ten' – have become part of our day-to-day language.

I'd been competing in quizzes myself since I was eighteen so I knew how lucrative and important they could be to a pub. I'd had a glimpse of it at The Greenfield when Sarah and I were running their quiz. So I had put a lot of thought into the one I was now running at The Crown.

I'd developed my own personal quizmaster style at The Greenfield. I didn't turn up in a spangly jacket or with a chip on my shoulder. I didn't try to imitate whoever was popular on the TV at the time, whether it was Chris Tarrant from *Who Wants to Be a Millionaire?* or Anne Robinson from *The Weakest Link*. I was just Jay. With all my quirks and flaws, of which there were plenty. I frequently fluffed lines, mispronounced things and made other howling errors. But that was my natural style. It seemed to go down well.

As someone who had played a lot of pub quizzes over the years, I knew a few things were key. The first was that familiar holy grail – loyalty. I needed to get the same people coming back week in, week out. There was a good reason for this. I knew that teams enjoy playing against the same opposition. They enjoy pitting their wits against people they know and engage with. It leads to a rivalry but, more importantly, to a sense of community. It helps make sure people have a good time. Which was the other important ingredient.

From my own days as a quiz participant, I knew that pub quizzes can actually be dull. I've been to several that were repetitive and basically not a lot of fun. They weren't helped by quizmasters whose hearts simply weren't in it. They'd read the questions out as if they were reading a shopping list or placing a takeaway order on the phone.

So I mixed things up from the beginning. At the end of each Thursday night, for instance, I introduced a one-off 'snowball' question in which a jackpot was accumulated each week. If someone got it right, they won the cash prize; if no one got it right, the money would roll forward and be added to the following week's prize. I didn't want people to win the snowball when it was a relatively small amount, so I made the questions pretty much impossible to begin with. What's the distance from Pluto to Neptune? That kind of thing. Professor Brian Cox didn't generally bring a team of astrophysicists into Darwen on Thursdays. But as the weeks went by and the money accumulated, I eased up. How many people died when the *Titanic* sank? There were people who knew that kind of thing. At one point, the snowball had grown to almost £500 – a lot of money.

I also mixed it up by introducing game-show-style elements into the quiz. This was something I'd done back at The Greenfield as well. I'd introduced a kind of *Deal or No Deal* element where the winning team was able to gamble their winnings at the end of the night by choosing from a number of boxes. Some contained booby prizes, but one contained a jackpot. It had worked well.

At The Crown, I'd invite a member of each team up to try solo rounds, say five questions on geography. It kept teams on their toes but also generated a lot of excitement – and fun.

That was something that was really important to me. The Thursday quiz was a big part of some people's social life. There were teams who, just like my old friends from the motor trade, used the quiz as a way of ensuring they got together regularly. There were other players who, I knew, only came out that one night of the week. It was their outlet, their escape from the stresses and strains of their domestic or work life. There were those who simply loved the challenge of the quiz. And that idea of being right, at least for an hour or two each week. It really was quite a diverse crowd, for Darwen at least. I wasn't there to psychoanalyse or judge them. I was there to give them an entertaining evening. And to make them feel welcome.

With that in mind, I tried my best to establish a rapport. I always made sure to mingle during the half-time break, for instance. I'd chat with the teams, especially the new arrivals or the 'floating voters' who turned up sporadically, repeating questions if they were having trouble. If it was a team that wasn't in serious contention for winning the quiz, I might even give them a hint as to the answer. It didn't do any harm. Similarly, if there were people in the pub who were playing the quiz alone, I'd get them to join other teams. No one minded.

Crucially, I also engaged with the teams that gave me a hard time. Hecklers are part and parcel of pub quizzes and I didn't mind them at all. People are always going to argue that their answers were close enough to merit a point or that, in fact, my answer was completely wrong. The key thing was to engage with them in a light-hearted and fair way. Turn it into a joke, even better a running gag if you could. It all helped to generate that all-important fun factor.

My frequent *faux pas* actually helped in that respect. I was never allowed to forget one of them, a blunder I made during an audio round. I'd recorded a series of famous voices, which the quizzers would have to identify. I'd been distracted by something or other and played the final voice in the round. I'd then said: 'BBC Radio 1 DJ Andi Peters there. So whose voice was that?' The place erupted into howls of laughter. I never lived that one down. My friends Haydn, Gareth, Roy, Ryan, Ste and Sal even renamed their team 'The Return of Andi Peters'. Someone told me later that I'd become known as the least professional quizmaster in Darwen. It was a badge of honour as far as I was concerned. It meant I'd connected with people. And I'd stood out from the crowd.

It all paid dividends. The number of teams playing our quiz grew and grew. At one point we had close to a dozen teams of four or five people competing each Thursday. On a few occasions, we were so full we had to pack people into the adjacent pool room or ask teams to stand at the bar. Quiz players began to appear in the pub on other nights of the week as well. So, like my jackpot question, it snowballed. What was particularly gratifying for me was that I became friendly with many of the players. I recall one team were off on holiday to the United States. It had always been a dream of mine to visit America, New York in particular. As an aside, I'd said: 'Bring me back a one-dollar note to prove you were there.' Sure enough, when they returned from their holiday, they handed me a crisp note. I was really touched. It meant a lot to me.

*

The summer of 2019 was fairly successful, boosted by the town's annual music festival, which I made sure we were plugged into. The pub was packed for some of the gigs we staged that summer. I also came up with a few other attractions. We had movie nights, put on a special night to watch the final episode of *Game of Thrones* on the big projector screen. But our takings just weren't at the level we needed to keep us afloat. As we headed towards the all-important Christmas and New Year period, I knew it was make or break. Our Christmas was a relative success. But as we moved through December, I knew that New Year's Eve 2019 was the big turning point for me. We had to have an absolutely bumper night if we were going to survive. It was one of the biggest nights – if not *the* biggest – of the year for pubs and was made all the more important by the fact that the rest of January was always dead.

Sarah had joined me to give a helping hand. Her mum was more than happy to babysit Jack. Sarah knew what was riding on the night. We'd made the decision not to charge an entry fee, which was unusual. Most pubs in town charged a sometimes hefty fee. We drew a big crowd, most of whom stayed for the midnight celebrations and beyond. I had some live music and provided a bit of food. People had a good time.

Sarah, Paige and I stayed on after we'd cleared up and had a few drinks with some close friends. I'd done a quick check of the till and run the numbers. We'd done well but not well enough to make up for all those days and nights when the pub was empty. New Year's Eve and especially the following day is a time when everyone naturally takes stock. When you project forward to the future. As hard as I tried, I couldn't see much of one at The Crown. I had a feeling the writing was on the wall.

In early January I made one last attempt to change things, suggesting to our area manager that we be freed from our 'tied' obligations in return for a higher rent. By now, I'd worked out that I could save massive amounts by buying in beer and other alcohol from other sources. I could buy barrels of lager at less than half what I was currently paying. It would be worth paying a higher rent to have that freedom. But I was told it was a non-starter.

I knew there was a clause that allowed us to break the three-year contract we'd signed at the end of the first twelve months. Sarah, Paige and I discussed it and we were in agreement. We told the management company to look for an alternative landlord. If nothing had changed by April, we'd have to activate the break clause and hand back the keys.

A part of me still clung to the hope that I could find a solution. Pull off some magic trick that would transform everything. I still had one mad idea up my sleeve.

The fact that we couldn't use the upstairs room had always gnawed away at me. It seemed such a waste of a great space. But then I had a brainwave. Escape rooms were gaining in popularity around the country. I knew for a fact that Darwen didn't have one. So I began revamping the room and working on puzzles and games that people would need to solve in order to find the keys secreted in the locked room and escape.

I was excited. If it took off . . . who knew? I might just pull the rabbit out of the hat.

I tried to get the local press interested but they wouldn't bite. I even enlisted our MP again, but he couldn't really help this time. Early on we had a couple of bookings, one from some friends and another one from some locals looking for a different way to celebrate a birthday. But without any options to give it serious promotion, it didn't take off.

I wasn't going to be defeated easily. So in an attempt to build some excitement – and more sales – I had another brilliant idea. The pub was fitted with CCTV cameras, one of which was trained on our stage for some unknown reason. I moved it up to the escape room so that people in the main bar downstairs could watch what was going on upstairs on a monitor. It would provide some entertainment – and more importantly, encourage others to have a go in the escape room.

I'd always been a little bit accident prone. Somehow, in the act of removing the camera, I managed to stab myself in the hand with a pair of scissors. It wasn't just a nick – the scissors penetrated right through my hand. Only the bone stopped the blade coming out the other side. It really hurt and I lost a lot of blood. The local A & E told me I'd severed tendons and nerves and that I might not get feeling back in my hand, which turned out to be true.

The accident put me out of action for a while. I was forced to sit at home on the sofa, watching TV and stewing on the fate of the pub. Not that it was in much doubt. My escape plan had failed. As we approached the end of January 2020, I had begun to accept the inevitable. Something extraordinary would have to happen if I was going to remain the landlord of The Crown. As it happens, something extraordinary did happen. And it proved decisive in a way I could never have predicted.

★

The first we'd heard of the coronavirus had been in the middle of the month, when there had been a couple of news items on the TV. The Foreign Office had issued a warning against British people travelling to the city of Wuhan, where the outbreak seemed to have started. Then British Airways suspended all flights to China.

In the pub, the news was greeted with not much more than a shrug and a bit of politically incorrect banter. 'Shouldn't be eating bats, should they?' someone said one evening as we watched the TV. It was a pub, not Twitter – we couldn't kick someone out for off-colour humour.

But then, right at the end of the month, the first two cases of the virus in the UK were discovered in York. The mood changed. The virus had arrived in England, the north of England to be precise, just a few hours' drive away from us. Suddenly, everyone began to take it seriously.

During my confinement to the sofa, I spent a lot of time watching the rolling news and could see the way it was heading. The virus seemed to have hit Italy particularly hard and the government there was already talking about closing down its economy and locking up its populace. It seemed to me inevitable that something similar would happen here.

So when the management company got back to me and said they'd found a new landlord to take over at the beginning of March, I was quietly relieved. It meant we only had to survive February. I didn't envy them the task that lay ahead. The more I watched the news, the more certain I became that I'd dodged a bullet.

The number of confirmed cases of the coronavirus in the UK was slowly ticking up. The news ran stories of people being trapped on cruise liners, confined to their cabins for days, sometimes weeks. There was more and more talk of international borders being closed. Airlines grounding their planes. New words and phrases were entering the language, almost on a weekly basis. Pandemic. Contact tracing. PPE. The virus was now known as COVID-19.

I was closer to it than most. Sarah wasn't at the front line of the NHS – she was an administrator, organising care for lymphoedema and similar blood circulation issues – but she did share her clinic with doctors, paramedics and nurses who were ramping up in readiness. She'd arrive home from work talking about the new rules, working practices and overtime schedules that were being introduced. Sarah is one of the world's most laid-back people, but I could tell that even she was getting anxious. It was clear that things were escalating – and fast. It was no longer if but when. We were in the calm before the storm.

We began clearing out of The Crown in the first week of March. We'd been in charge for eleven months. It was a bittersweet moment. I'd shed blood, sweat and tears. Literally, in the case of my hand, which was still heavily bandaged. Part of me felt aggrieved, like I'd not been given a fair crack of the whip. But also that I'd been naive. That feeling only deepened when, to my annoyance, the new landlords turned up to prepare for their arrival before we'd even left. I'd hoped not to cross paths with them. I felt sore. A part of me felt like I'd messed up, that I was a loser. I didn't want to see some wise guy or girl come in and tell me where I'd gone wrong. Or, even worse, boast of the new plans they had for the place. Which, as it turned out, was exactly what happened.

The owners had given the new landlords a deal that meant they weren't 'tied' to the company as I'd been and were free to buy their own stock. This really irritated me. Why couldn't they have given me that opportunity?

I tried to temper my anger by looking at the reality. They were going to be taking the pub over at a time of huge uncertainty. During that last week, the first death from COVID in the UK had been announced and the Prime Minister had hinted at what he called 'a substantial period of disruption where we have to deal with this outbreak'. Anyone who had been paying attention knew what that meant. The signs were already there. Fewer and fewer people were going out. Within the trade, there was talk of all pubs and restaurants being closed down completely. The storm was drawing closer.

The final days of the pub were emotional. To avoid having to answer a million questions – and to protect my wounded pride a little too – we'd told our regulars that the owners had independently decided to install a new landlord. It was partially true.

My quiz regulars were the most upset about the news. For some of them, I knew, it was one of the highlights of their week. So when I ran the final Thursday night quiz, we went out in style. I made sure the jackpot question was won and was generous with spot prizes of free drinks for people who got particular questions right.

There was a hard core of quizzers with whom I'd become really friendly. The team that had christened itself The Return of Andi Peters was among them. I assured them that they'd see me around town, playing alongside them in other quizzes. I'd even heckle the quizmasters in the way they'd regularly – and light-heartedly – teased me. I also told them they'd be the first to know if and when someone let me run a new quiz in town. At the back of my mind, I had a faint hope that might happen one day, but it seemed a distant prospect that night.

I was close to tears at various points during the evening, but I really struggled to keep it together when I got to the final question. I thought it would be the last I'd ever ask as a quizmaster. It was certainly one of the easiest.

'Name this song,' I said, then sang along to the opening lines of Frank Sinatra's 'New York, New York'. 'Start spreading the news, I'm leaving today.'

I couldn't have known it then, of course, but I was doing something of a Sinatra. Didn't he retire and then return to the stage half a dozen times?

★

The final day at The Crown was a strange and unsettling experience.

Paige didn't have anywhere to move on to, so Sarah and I had offered her a spare room in our house until she found a new flat in town. There was no way I was going to leave her homeless. It was the least we could do. Despite my insistence that we make monthly repayments, the loan she'd taken on to finance the pub hadn't been cleared. I wasn't going to walk away from my responsibilities to that. It would take us a while to sort it out.

So we spent the first part of the day loading her stuff into my car. She was quite emotional too, even though she knew, like me, we were doing the right thing. It just felt sad. We'd had some great times. Created something special, we thought.

The new landlords were already busy moving their stuff in. With everything packed up, I handed back the keys, wished them best of luck, grabbed a few final bits and pieces that belonged to me and stepped out of the pub into the street.

It was eerily quiet, with only a few vehicles on the road and hardly anyone out and about. You could hear the crows in the trees. It felt like the world was shutting down.

Driving home, Paige and I sat in silence, each of us lost in our private thoughts. I could tell she was still upset, and worried. It was only natural.

I felt the same way.

At the most basic level, I was worried about Sarah and Jack and their future now that our main livelihood had gone. The coronavirus situation hardly helped.

But I also knew myself well enough to recognise the other emotions that were churning around. Familiar ones. Unwelcome ones.

I'd taken a big gamble and it hadn't come off. I felt disappointment, rejection, failure, anger, regret. I felt let down too, as if I'd been too trusting of others. My pride and, yes, my ego had been hurt. All of those feelings were gathering into a dark cloud that I could sense looming above me. I was beginning to feel isolated, lonely. I was starting to wonder where and how I fitted into the world. I was feeling lost. Again . . .

2

ASK NO QUESTIONS . . .

In the Harry Potter books, who is referred
to as the 'chief Death Eater'?
The Harry Potter specialist round
in Jay's Virtual Pub Quiz Book 2

Betamax was the rival to which video format?
Jay's Virtual Pub Quiz No 6, March 2020

SW19 is the postcode for which tennis tournament?
Jay's Virtual Pub Quiz No 4, March 2020

Which company is associated with the
advertising slogan 'I'm lovin' it'?
Jay's Virtual Pub Quiz No 16, June 2020

Most childhoods are filled with an endless stream of questions. Why this? Why that? Are we there yet?

Mine was no different. I suspect I asked more than most. Within my family, however, I didn't always get the answers. We had secrets. Subjects that weren't to be broached. There was nothing particularly unusual in that, of course. All families are the same. We all have our skeletons in the closet. The problem was that, in my case, it made me a little boy who was insecure about himself. Who struggled to work out who he was, and how

– or where – he fitted into the world. No matter how hard he tried.

I was born in south London in 1982. My mum, Dawn, was very young, a week or two shy of her seventeenth birthday, when I arrived in the world. By the time she was eighteen, she'd given birth to my sister, Natalie. There were just thirteen months between us.

As a young boy, I didn't know my dad at all. That was one of the big no-go areas when it came to asking questions. I remember how, if his name came up, there were tuts and scowls, rolls of the eyes and shakes of the head. He was a bit like Voldemort in the Harry Potter books. His name couldn't be mentioned.

According to the family narrative, my mum left him after he smashed a window in their small ground-floor council flat in Colliers Wood near Wimbledon, leaving broken glass in the cot that I or my sister was sleeping in. He'd crossed a line. She'd packed her bags. I had no reason to disbelieve it when I was growing up. I only had one version of events. And it was being delivered by the people that I loved and trusted most in the world.

We went to live with my mum's parents, my grandparents, in a large house in a leafy Edwardian terrace on Farquhar Road, in Wimbledon Park. Looking back on my early years, there's no question in my mind – my time there was the happiest of my childhood.

The house was in London, but it really didn't feel like it. The All England Lawn Tennis Club was no more than half a mile away and when the wind was blowing in the right direction during Wimbledon fortnight, you could hear the cheers from Centre Court. My grandma used to joke that those two weeks were the one time of the year when she had a personalised weather forecast on the TV. She'd always have the tennis on and if she saw the covers being put up to protect the courts from rain, she'd know to head into the garden and bring in her washing.

It was a close community. Not grand in any way, certainly not like the same street today, filled with million-pound houses and fancy cars. The house had an old-fashioned gas and electric meter that we'd have to ram fifty-pence pieces into when the lights went out. The garden had an old Second World War Anderson shelter, which had been sealed and then covered up with soil. Buried. I'd have loved to have been able to play inside it. I imagined gas masks, lamps, all the paraphernalia from the war still intact inside.

I can see now that the shelter symbolised the household in more ways than one. My grandparents were both from the generation that grew up before and during the Second World War. They epitomised the spirit of the generation who had hidden in their Anderson shelters during the Blitz. They had that blend of quiet determination and optimism that came from living through rationing and all the deprivations of the war. Unfortunately for me, like that underground shelter, they also came from a generation that kept things buried. Emotions especially.

My grandma, Esme, was a character and a half. She was from a Welsh family and was short, red-haired, and fiery at times. She smoked sixty cigarettes a day, enjoyed a glass of whisky, and spent as many of her evenings as she could manage playing bingo at the local venue in Wimbledon. She had a heart of pure gold and was generous to a fault. I can still remember the prizes she brought us kids home from bingo. Stuffed toys and board games. Cheap 'knock-off' versions of more successful games. Drainpipes and scaffolding rather than snakes and ladders! We played them all though. As well as games like Yahtzee, which my gran taught me and I loved.

My gran worked at a local supermarket for a while. But when she was home she spent most of her time in the kitchen, cooking, cleaning, singing or whistling to herself. I remember regular visits from people she'd pay for catalogues or Christmas clubs. She was constantly hiding things away 'for Christmas', her favourite time of the year. I can see now that my mum was still very young when I was growing up, still in her early twenties. She'd been forced to move back in with her parents while dealing with a marital break-up and two young children. That can't have been easy. She would have been all over the place emotionally. So it was my gran who was the reliable rock, the homemaker who made sure we were all cared for. As a little boy, I needed her. I needed my grandad even more though.

My grandad, Christopher, was a south Londoner born and bred and had been a teenager during the early days of the Second World War. He used to tell a story that he was cycling around the neighbourhood in Wimbledon Park when a German aeroplane flew over and shot him in the backside. My mum always thought it was a tall tale for us grandchildren. It certainly made us roll around with laughter whenever he told it. He served briefly in the army very late in the war, so missed the worst of the action.

He'd spent most of his working life in the cinema business, first as a projectionist for ABC cinemas, then as a manager for the Cannon Cinemas chain. He moved up from that to be the company's booking agent, basically deciding which films went in which of their cinemas. He was a real film afficionado and the house was filled with VHS cassettes. He even had his own editing equipment for splicing together old Super 8 films. My grandad was in his late fifties when I was born, so by the time I was seven or so, he was approaching retirement age. As his career had entered its twilight years, I suppose it was natural that he lived a lot of his life vicariously through his children and grandchildren, and in particular me. As far as I was concerned, he was my father. He saw things that way too and treated me as his son. Most of the happy memories I have of my childhood are of spending time with him.

I'd spend holidays and weekends travelling around with him. He'd often take me into meetings with the big film executives in Soho Square. He'd slip me into private screenings of films. I felt like a VIP, sitting in the plush velvety seats, sometimes just the two of us, while the projectionist ran a movie for us.

Given all this, he got very excited when, for a time, it looked like I might follow him into the cinema business. On the screen, rather than behind it.

★

With the benefit of hindsight, I can see now why I became a child actor. It's a bit of a cliché in a way. I was a sensitive, slightly repressed little boy. There was clearly a lot going on inside my young head. I had a lot of emotions and energy that needed an outlet. Acting provided it.

My mum and grandparents weren't psychologists, however. So, for them, it came completely out of the blue.

As far as they were concerned, I'd just been a quiet, introverted boy. There were none of the usual signs. I'd not been one of those attention-seeking kids who always performed at family get-togethers. I'd not been one to rummage around in the household wardrobes to find fancy dress outfits. It had all come out when I'd appeared in a nativity play at my school, Wimbledon Park Primary. I'd played the star that appeared over Bethlehem. Apparently, my mum and grandparents were thrilled and shocked in equal measure. They barely recognised the person on the stage. There is a video of it somewhere. I've never had the courage to look at it.

To their credit, my mum and grandparents recognised what I needed. My aunt somehow got the number of a talent agency that represented a neighbour's daughter and had got her a big part in *EastEnders*. I was soon being put up for advertising, stage and TV roles.

I can only assume that I had a bit of talent at that point, or appealed to casting companies in some way. According to my grandad, they had been told by the agency that it would take a hundred auditions to get a job. I landed one in ten. I was signed up for an advert for Woolworth's, the high street retail chain. I still have a copy of it. I'm in school uniform and have a mass of curls. People tell me I look cute, but that's for them to say. Again, I find it hard to look.

Work in other ads followed. I was also auditioned for TV and theatre roles.

My grandad's influence came to the fore again. He had his generation's attitude to work. 'Put in the graft and you'll get the rewards.' So he taught me to treat it all seriously. To be polite, punctual, learn my lines and listen to what I was told by the casting directors. It seemed to pay off. I was cast as the young Macduff in a high-profile new production of *Macbeth* at the Riverside Studios in Hammersmith.

That was when I really did start to take it seriously.

I was taken under the wing of Cathy Shipton, a successful TV actress. She was a maternal figure in the production. She taught me how to project my voice in a theatre without shouting. She was so patient and supportive; she'd spend hours guiding and coaching me.

I'd clearly developed some confidence by then because I recall asking the director why myself and the two other boys who played the role on rotation because of our age weren't invited out for the curtain call at the end of each show. He said I was welcome to do so and so I did. At every performance. I was getting the bug.

The other thrill was meeting famous people. Brian May from Queen had written the score for the production and appeared at the theatre one day. He gave me a cassette of the score and signed a dedication to me. I was completely starstruck.

The acting profession is all about momentum. One thing tends to lead to another. Which is what happened to me. I got cast in a string of other roles, including in a couple of films, *Paper Mask* with Paul McGann and Amanda Donohoe and *The Comfort of Strangers* with Christopher Walken, Helen Mirren, Rupert Everett and Natasha Richardson. I didn't make the final cut in that one, but my grandad somehow got hold of a still from the production to prove I'd been part of the cast.

At that point, the acting world seemed a really welcoming place. The adult actors I worked with were invariably kind to me.

Cathy Shipton was particularly good to me and recommended me for a part in *Casualty*, the BBC's long-running medical drama. I played a boy called Jamie in an episode called 'Hide and Seek' in the sixth season of the drama and went to Bristol for a few days' filming, I recall. That was in the autumn of 1991. I was nine. It was then that I had my big chance.

Every aspiring actor – even a nine-year-old one – is looking for the breakthrough role, the part or show that changes their life. In 1991, I was auditioned for a new TV programme called *2point4 Children*. It was a comedy about a typical family with – in line with the well-known statistic – two point four children. The joke was that as well as the two children – a brother and sister – the father, played by Gary Olsen, was a bit of a child himself. It was clearly a show with potential. I auditioned a few times for the role of the son and got down to the final two, along with a young actor called John Pickard. I don't recall why they went so far with me, because John was a few years older. Maybe they were experimenting with children of different ages. I don't know. But in the end John got the role in the series, which went on to become a big hit on the BBC, pulling in an audience of nearly ten million and running for eight series over the next eight years.

Looking back on it, I can see that it must have been a turning point for me. Who knows how my future would have played out if I'd been cast? Maybe I could have gone on to establish myself in the same way as John, who had a successful TV career? My life might have gone down a completely different path. The issues that were already beginning to affect me may not have developed. Who knows? All I do know is that it didn't happen for me. And my life took the direction that it did.

My mum and grandparents had protected me from a lot of the rejections that came routinely with acting. They were conscious, I suspect, that I had already suffered a massive rejection from my father. In my child's-eye view of the world, he didn't want anything to do with me. We saw and heard nothing of him. But there was no concealing the disappointment everyone felt when I missed out on the *2point4 Children* role. My mum and grandparents had been very excited at the prospect of me starring in a big TV show. My missing out was a blow to them too.

My memories of that moment are foggy, but it must have hurt me. Apart from anything else, it would have undermined that lesson my grandad had drilled into me. Hard work brought results. I'd always been someone who tried hard. Who gave his all. Discovering that effort and enthusiasm wasn't always enough must have been a blow. Confusing too. The reason I say this is that I know acting began to lose its appeal afterwards. In my mind, at least, it became less glamorous. More of a chore. Something I did to please others, especially my grandad, who was so proud of everything I did. By the time I reached my early teens, I'd left the agency. Life had become even more confusing by then.

After the break-up of her marriage to my dad, my mum had to rebuild her life while trying to raise two children. It took its toll, I think. I can now see how much of a struggle it must have been. My memory of her is her working non-stop. She'd done a stint in a supermarket where my gran had also worked, but also at the local Blockbuster video store, which involved a lot of night and weekend shifts. I don't know whether it was my grandad's influence that landed her the job.

I remember her going out every now and again. She was still in her twenties when I was a young boy. It was only natural. She had a couple of boyfriends but then started a more serious relationship with a local guy called Simon.

Looking back on it, I can see that must have caused me issues. I already felt that I didn't get a lot of attention. It was why, I can see now, I was always looking for her approval. I suspect it was one of the reasons, subconsciously, why I'd thrown myself into acting, an environment entirely built on approval, or applause to be precise. With my mum now committed to a new relationship, I became more difficult. I'd developed an independent streak. I could be wilful and defiant too. I wouldn't listen. To her, at least. My grand-parents were different. I suppose they gave me the attention I craved. I sense that I respected them a little more, for whatever reason.

My behaviour began to get worse and me and my mum started to clash. Not violently; we just rubbed each other up the wrong way. There were tantrums, slammed doors. Lots of walking off in a huff.

The situation was probably exacerbated by my sister. Natalie and I didn't get on particularly well. We'd often argue. The distance between us grew when she also began to dominate my mum's atten-tion. My sister had dabbled with acting too, but had become most successful as a trampoline gymnast and had to be ferried around to assorted competitions most weekends, sometimes outside London and in other parts of the country. I'd spend a lot of time with my grandad when they were out of town. We'd occasionally go to watch Wimbledon FC, who were doing really well at the time, getting promoted to the old first division and then the Premier League. But I felt disconnected from my mum and my sister. That distance only grew when I suffered a trauma that I'd never fully share with them. It's remained locked behind the steel doors of my repressed child-hood memories ever since. It was then that I was left in the care of a friend of the family, who sexually abused me.

It wasn't always possible for me to spend weekends with my grandparents. They were elderly and needed a break at times. So my mum had agreed that occasionally I'd stay with relatives. We had an aunt I liked who lived in nearby New Malden, with some cous-ins. But I also began to spend Saturdays with a single, middle-aged guy who had become friendly with the family. My grandparents, mum and aunt knew a lot of people locally and he was part of their social circle. He'd befriended me and would take me out for a burger, a real treat for me at the time. He seemed to share some of my interests. Films, video games. He was the kind of grown-up male company that, I guess, I'd been missing. He was from the generation after my grandad. Of course, from the perspective of today, I can see how completely inappropriate it was. Alarm bells should have been ringing all over the place. I was nine at the time. Completely innocent. I didn't see anything sinister or threatening in his behaviour. And if the adults in my life said it was OK, I assumed it was. Somehow, he'd got them to agree to me staying over at his flat a few miles away from where we lived. They obviously trusted him. They couldn't have known what he was really like.

During my stays there, he'd put me up on a camp bed in his living room while he slept in his own room. He'd drink heavily. He also showed me inappropriate material on a computer that he owned.

I'd begun to feel more and more uncomfortable. And then, one Saturday night while I was staying there, he climbed into my camp bed. I remember his breath stank of booze.

I won't spell out what happened exactly, but it crossed the line. I was very young and, looking back on it, I think I simply blanked it out. I pretended it wasn't happening – and, afterwards, that it had never happened. I certainly didn't tell anyone about it. I was too confused, ashamed and upset. My relations with my mum weren't great. I was convinced she wouldn't believe me if I told her about it. He'd obviously deny it and blame it on my overdramatic persona. I was acting. So deep down, even though his connection to the family hadn't begun with her, I ended up blaming my mum for it. For abandoning me to him.

Somehow, I managed to ensure that I was never left alone with him after that. I certainly never stayed there again. His interest in looking after me disappeared. I tried to spend more time watching the football at Wimbledon with my grandad. Emotionally, however, it wasn't easy to move on. I had no one to talk to. I could never, in a million years, have broached the subject with my grandad. I was forced to carry that burden around with me.

Inevitably, I suppose, I began to play up more and more. The signs were there; I was becoming a really messed-up kid. So it perhaps wasn't much of a surprise when I decided to run away from home.

I'd had an argument with my sister. I'd been accused of something I felt was unfair, to do with the Nintendo gaming system that I used to play a little too often for my mum's liking. I'd clearly wanted my departure to be as dramatic as possible, so I had written a note explaining that I was leaving home and was 'never, ever coming back'. I'd added, pointedly, that Natalie could have my Nintendo as far as I was concerned. I'd then packed a bag, left the note at the bottom of the stairs and headed out. I remember it was a Sunday, around 7 p.m. I walked alongside the railway line from Wimbledon Park through Wimbledon town centre, heading towards New Malden where my cousins and aunt lived. I'm not sure why I headed there, and I wasn't planning on staying. It was simply a route I knew. It was a long walk, especially for a young child. I got as far as nearby Dundonald Park. By now it was dark and getting scary. The shadows were lengthening. There weren't many people about. When I spotted a telephone box, I made a reverse charge phone call home. My grandad answered. He told me to stay put. My mum was at work and had to ask for an hour off. She belted over to pick me up and gave me the biggest telling-off I'd ever had as we drove back in the car. When I got home, I found my letter was still sitting on the stairs. No one had even seen it. So much for my grandiose gesture.

Looking back now, I guess it was a textbook reaction. I was a young boy who'd never known his father and felt rejected by his absence. A distance had developed between me and my mother and sister. I wasn't particularly successful at school. I suffered regular rejections as an actor. And then I'd been abused by a predator and partly blamed my mother for it. It was little wonder that I began to have severe trust issues. Not just at home but with the entire world.

It didn't get any easier as I moved into my teens.

I was in middle school when my mother decided to move out of my grandparents' house and live with Simon. My sister and I moved with her to Morden, a few miles away from Wimbledon. I became more independent, travelling back and forth to my new school,

Tamworth Manor, on the bus each day. I'd continue to visit my grandparents as often as possible. However, slowly but surely, my sense of isolation began to grow. I didn't get on well with Simon, even though I attended the Sea Cadets where he was the senior officer. The fact that we lived under the same roof counted for nothing. I felt that he picked on me more than anyone else. A part of me didn't trust him, but then I didn't trust anyone apart from my grandparents at that point, especially adult male figures.

When I was twelve, my mum and Simon had a child together, a little brother, Conor. He was lovely and I could see that it made my mother happy. But it pushed me even further down the pecking order.

My mum's new life put a distance between her and my grandparents too. When she and Simon got married a year or so after Conor was born, they had a 'secret' ceremony where only a handful of people were invited. My grandparents hadn't been included but then – bizarrely – my mum and Simon had a party that night to which they, and other friends and family members, were invited to hear the big, surprise news. I can still see the heartbreak on my grandad's face when he was told his daughter had got married without him being there. My grandad was my idol. Seeing him hurt made me feel terrible.

I think it all contributed to me becoming a more distant and introverted boy.

My new school didn't help much.

Switching schools was always a challenge. I found it hard to make new friends. I was still a trier, however, and did my best to fit in, forming a few close friendships. It was here that acting came to my aid.

Puberty was kicking in by now, of course. The issue of what girls thought of me had become crucially important. I had enjoyed the attention when I was a younger actor but now I was a typical self-conscious teenager. Probably more self-conscious than most, given the experience I'd had with the family friend. But I took the view that acting would at least increase my popularity at school. I wasn't a sporty child so it was the one area where I could excel.

The professional attitude I'd learned years earlier helped. Towards the end of my time at Tamworth Manor, I landed the plum comic role of Bottom in the school production of Shakespeare's *A Midsummer Night's Dream*. But on the day of the opening night, I tried an overambitious move on the basketball court and landed really badly on my knee. For a moment I think they were worried I'd smashed it, so my mum was called to school and I was ferried off to hospital. Luckily, it was OK and I was discharged in time to get back to school for the performance. I arrived on stage on crutches – to a rousing round of applause. It was probably the highlight of my entire time there.

It coincided with a brief revival of my interest in professional acting. Around this time, my school formed a link to the production company behind the popular TV police drama *The Bill*, which was filmed nearby in Wimbledon. A few of us were invited to audition to be part of the show's workshop programme. The idea was for them to develop a pool of local child actors they could tap into as and when needed. I was one of the kids chosen.

Unlike most of the kids, who performed background or extras roles, I did manage to land a decent part in the show. I was beyond excited when I starred in an episode playing a tearaway who had a run-in with PC George Garfield, played by the actor Huw Higginson. We had a fight scene in which I had to kick him in the nether regions. I was reluctant. It didn't seem right, but Huw was a really great guy and kept reassuring me it was OK. My grandad had always taught me to listen to authority figures like policemen, so I went along with his orders. It all contributed to my studies back at school, where I did well in drama. Unfortunately, the same couldn't be said about the rest of the curriculum.

I wasn't unintelligent. I just had issues with concentration and – well – boredom. I wanted to be active and doing stuff, not sitting reading and writing essays. So I tended to drift off into my imagination during lessons. That was always a place where I felt safe. I fantasised about being Michael Schumacher at the wheel of a Formula One car. Or playing for Spurs, the football team I'd adopted now that I was no longer going to watch Wimbledon. No one really noticed. My underwhelming results were taken at face value. As far as the school was concerned, I just wasn't an A-stream kid.

Having said that, I must have shown some creative promise because I was invited on a weekend away for so-called 'gifted and talented' children. It wasn't the most inspirational trip and the only thing I remember was having to come up with our own board game. I'd loved board games since I used to play snakes and ladders and Yahtzee with my grandmother, so it suited me right down to the ground.

But it was a rare highlight.

My school years were summed up in a way by a moment during my final year, when I was in the fifth form. We were having our final lesson in, I think, history, and – for some reason – I mentioned to the teacher that, unlike most of my schoolmates, I'd never been dismissed from a class during my time there. It wasn't much of a boast, obviously. Nevertheless, the teacher decided that I needed to leave the classroom and stand outside for the rest of the lesson, 'just to see what it's like'. He said it with a smile on his face. It was meant as a joke, but looking back it really encapsulated my time at school. Aside from my appearances on the stage, I'd not really made much of a mark. One way or the other. I might as well have spent my entire time there in the corridor.

The inevitable consequence was that I left school with an unimpressive list of GCSEs. My highest mark was a B in drama.

I briefly attended a local further education college hoping to do an A level in drama that might lead to work in the theatre or film industry, but I was required to do two other subjects. I started a GNVQ in business studies and Spanish, of all things. It really didn't suit me, and by the end of the first half term I'd decided to drop out.

*

My mum wasn't massively pleased about it, but agreed I could leave if I found a job. There was a new McDonald's opening in Wimbledon town centre, and they were recruiting. It might not have been my dream job, but it was definitely better than staying at college. When they told me I was hired, it felt like a huge weight had been lifted off my shoulders. I was free. Free to be me. Whoever he was.

I knew one thing about myself. The work ethic I'd developed as a child actor meant that I wasn't afraid to put in the hours and the effort. And as I settled into the job, I enjoyed it. The pay packet I took home at the end of each month helped, of course. I felt able to be more independent. Self-sufficient, even financially. It was what I'd needed. For a while, at least. Long term, though, there was no hiding from the hard realities of life.

I'd already lost my grandmother. I'd known she was ill. All those years of smoking had taken their inevitable toll and she'd developed lung cancer. She'd stopped working and had become weaker, a shadow of her former dynamic self. She seemed to shrink every time I popped round to see her.

One day in January 1997, when I was fifteen, I'd come out from school and found my mum sitting near the gates in a car with Simon. She never picked me up from school, so I knew instantly there was something wrong and put two and two together.

It hit my grandad hard. They'd been together for forty years or more. But he refused to show it to the world. I remember him telling me how important it was to keep a stiff upper lip when you were the head of a family. How you had to keep your true emotions under control. It was a very old-school, male outlook, of course, but it made an impression coming from him. And so that's what I did as well. I repressed my feelings. Buried them like that Anderson shelter in their garden. Again.

I remember when the eulogy was read out at the funeral, I just wanted to sob my eyes out and grieve for the wonderful woman who'd played such a big part in my young life. But I didn't. I stood there in my new black suit and black tie, shoulder to shoulder with my grandad. And toughed it out. I can see now how damaging it was, for both of us.

My grandad became a more fragile figure after my grandma's death. He carried on living in the old family house, but it became a bit of a mausoleum. Filled with memories. Rather sad ones.

He'd come and visit us regularly. He was still my mentor, the only person in the world to whom I looked for guidance and support. I trusted him in a way I'd never trusted anyone.

I was still doing well at work and had received a couple of pay rises and minor promotions. I had a plan to move out and get a place of my own as soon as I could afford it. But I wasn't getting too carried away. I knew I was a work in progress. I also knew I was going to rely on my grandad to guide me during my transition into adulthood. We often talked about how we'd celebrate me reaching my eighteenth birthday by going for a pint in a local pub together. It never happened.

It was December 1998, just under two years after my gran died. He'd come round to the house to see us on a Wednesday afternoon. I must have been on an evening shift at work. Or finished an early one. I'd been upstairs on a computer, fully engrossed playing a game. I'd registered his arrival, but I'd not gone down to see him. I guess I figured I'd see him at the weekend. I vividly recall him shouting 'see you soon' from the foot of the stairs as he left. I never saw him again.

He'd apparently gone home and had a massive heart attack that night. It was to be three days later, the following Saturday, that he was found dead in his bed.

I felt like my world had been shattered into a million tiny pieces. But just as I'd done with my grandmother, I bottled up my pain.

The funeral was a big affair. There must have been a couple of hundred people in attendance. We started with a procession from the old family house on Farquhar Road. I'd insisted on being one of the pallbearers who carried his coffin into the church. I felt it was the right thing to do. To take him to his final resting place. It was standing room only at the church, which was a real comfort. Afterwards, at the wake, most of the mourners seemed to make a beeline for me. They all said the same thing: if they could do anything to help me, all I had to do was ask. Throughout it all I tried to project stoicism, strength. That stiff upper lip that my grandad had taught me. Everyone was behaving as if I'd become the male head of the family. But, in reality, I was very far from that. I was still just an immature teenager. I was sixteen. Dealing with a maelstrom of emotions. Or not, in most cases. My assault by the family friend remained something I'd bottled up too. To my horror, he turned up at the funeral, which churned things up inside me once more. I kept my distance, didn't make a scene. Fortunately, there were so many people there it was easy to avoid him.

It was an emotional crossroads for me. Inside, I was broken. Not for the first time, I felt like I'd been abandoned. My grandad had been everything to me. My father figure. My mentor. I looked up to him, admired him. And he'd left me too soon. I was an unfinished project. He hadn't fulfilled his mission of preparing me for the world. We hadn't had that pint together on my eighteenth birthday.

Of course, looking back on it, I can see that it wasn't unusual. Quite the opposite. People lose their grandparents. It's part of life. But I just wasn't ready for it, and I certainly wasn't equipped to deal with the whirl of emotions it stirred up within me. It brought all sorts of things to the surface. Things I couldn't handle. I felt utterly alone.

A light had been extinguished. It wasn't surprising that afterwards I spiralled into a dark new phase in my life.

3

FORTY PEOPLE IN DARWEN

'Just keep swimming' was said by which Disney animation character?
The Disney round in Jay's Virtual Pub Quiz Book 2

We all have days when our lives are tipped upside down. When everything changes and you know nothing will ever be the same again. Sometimes it happens in an instant and hits you like a bolt from the blue. That was how I felt when I learned my grandfather had died. My life was transformed in one painful flash. I knew the world would be a different place from then on.

But those life-changing moments can also creep up on you in slow motion. Without you realising what's really going on. That's what happened to me on Saturday 21 March 2020. It was the day that flipped my life on its head. But at the time it felt like just another really boring day at work.

★

During the final days at The Crown, I'd had to move fast. Sarah and I couldn't survive purely on her salary. I had to get another job. So I'd called Ian, my first boss in the motor trade, to see if he had any work. We'd remained on good terms and even attended each other's wedding. I counted him as a friend.

Ian had taken a chance on me seven or so years earlier when I'd never even attempted to sell a car. To my relief – and slight amazement – he said he was willing to take a chance again. It was March, normally one of the busiest months in the car sales calendar, and he was short-handed. I could start at the Suzuki dealership he now ran in Blackburn, a few miles away, in the third week of the month.

There was a caveat, of course. Ian hadn't remained a successful dealership manager by accident. The job offer was on condition I'd accept a smallish wage and base most of my income on the commission on sales. The more cars I sold, the more money I'd make. And vice versa. The fewer I sold, the less I'd take home at the end of the month. Beggars can't be choosers. I accepted the offer.

While I waited to start work I spent a week at home, looking after Jack and doing chores. I also helped Paige settle into our spare room and did odd bits of DIY around the house. The main job I wanted to tackle was a new playhouse for Jack in the rear garden of our four-bedroomed terrace house. He had a slide there, but he was rapidly outgrowing it. The timber and fittings for the playhouse were lying in a disorganised pile in our garden shed. Unfortunately, the wound to my hand still hadn't quite healed. I decided to put the task off until later in the spring.

I'd always tried to pull my weight when it came to the child-caring duties, so I didn't mind looking after Jack. He was three now and becoming a real chatterbox. I loved spending time with him at home or in the nearby park. Jack attended his nursery a short distance away four days a week, so it meant that I was left alone to twiddle my thumbs for a while. I'm not great at sitting around doing nothing, so by the end of the week I was climbing the walls. By the third Monday of March, the 16th, I was chomping at the bit to get started back at work.

I turned up, naturally feeling a little anxious. I had no idea about the specifications on the latest models that were glinting on the forecourt in the spring sunshine. So many new features and regulations had come in. EVs and hybrids were all the rage now. It was going to take me a while to get up to speed. I spent my first morning gobbling up as much information on the showroom's current range of cars as possible.

It was a lot to take in quickly, so when I encountered my first customer, I stuck to my old policy. No lies. No BS. I just told them that it was my first day, so they'd have to forgive any gaps in my knowledge. It didn't bother them. They bought a new car on the spot. I was so relieved. I'd made my first sale within hours.

Besides Ian, there were two other salesmen and a handful of support staff at the showroom. They all thought it was hilarious. One told me about a salesman who'd said it was his first day at work – every day for ten years. It was good to have the distraction and to have a laugh. There was a small TV in the showroom for customers. It was set permanently to the news. And it was getting bleak.

I'd known from Sarah that things were getting more and more serious at work as the number of COVID cases in the UK rose steadily. She'd told me that the really big concern was the breathing apparatus that was needed for those with severe cases of COVID. I'd seen horrific images of wards in hospitals in Italy where rows of patients were plugged into respirators. There was talk of giant NHS facilities being built inside football stadia to cope with potentially thousands of patients. The other big worry was the people who were most vulnerable – the elderly in care homes and those with what was being called 'a pre-existing condition'. People with cancer, breathing difficulties, that kind of thing. It made me worry more about Sarah. She suffers from narcolepsy and cataplexy, two related conditions that could lead her to drop off to sleep or lose muscle facility when she experiences strong emotions. Fortunately, she's ordinarily the most laid-back person in the world, and it's a problem she manages well thanks to medication. But these were extraordinary times. Everyone was sailing into uncharted waters. Tensions and emotions were going to run high. At least she was always surrounded by doctors and nurses. She was in the right place if, heaven forbid, something went wrong.

Sarah and her colleagues were already wearing PPE – protective clothing – at work, including masks and rubber gloves. Everything needed to be cleaned and sanitised to within an inch of its life. I knew exactly how that felt.

At work, we kept getting similar directives from head office. Surfaces had to be sanitised and wiped down after every contact. We had to try to avoid having too many of us inside the same space at the same time. We also had to stagger our tea or lunch breaks so as to maintain that other new term, social distancing.

As the week wore on, COVID and its new words and phrases became one of the few things we had to talk about. It was as quiet as the grave, so Ian got us to ring around prospective customers.

The message was the same. People were scared. They'd say: 'It's not really safe to go out.' Or: 'I'm not looking for a new car right now. Don't think I'll need one with what's coming.'

There really was a climate of fear. And it was growing.

By the end of my first week at the showroom, the mood was darkening even more. That Friday night, the Prime Minister, Boris Johnson, appeared on TV. He wasn't exactly the most popular person in the north-west of England before then, and the message he delivered didn't win him any new friends. He announced that all cafés, pubs, bars and restaurants were to close down tonight and wouldn't be opening again from tomorrow.

I watched the announcement on TV at home with Sarah. Within minutes, my phone began to buzz with messages from friends. A couple asked me if I wanted to go out that night to mark the rather gloomy occasion. That sounded like a particularly bad idea. I imagined a few pubs in town would be packed full of people, hell-bent on having one last wild night out. It would be an easy place to pick up COVID. I, for one, was taking the virus seriously and was certainly not going to put myself – and Jack and Sarah – in that position.

As the news sank in that evening, I couldn't help thinking about my old regulars in The Crown. For some of them, the pub was their only social outlet. Their only way of having some human interaction. For others, it was a haven. A place to get away from all their troubles. What would they do now? Where would they find those things? Some of them would be hit hard by this.

Closer to home, my other main concern was work. What was going to happen to the showroom? Ian rang me that evening to reassure me that he'd been given the green light to remain open. For the foreseeable future at least. There were no guarantees. The COVID situation was moving so fast that no one could predict anything. He told me I'd be working both days that weekend. So the following day, Saturday 21 March, I set off on the twenty-minute drive to Blackburn. It would be one of the most momentous days of my life. The day the earth moved. Day Zero. I certainly had zero idea what I'd set in motion.

★

Ordinarily, a Saturday is one of the busiest times of the week. It's a day car salesmen and women view with mixed feelings. There are a lot of sales prospects but also a lot of time wasters. People who come to see what we've got on display, often out of curiosity or boredom. They've no intention of buying a car. To be honest, that day I'd have loved to see dozens of time wasters. Once again, the place was like the deck of the *Marie Celeste*. We were told to work the phones and call existing customers. Invite them in for test drives. Hint at amazing deals available on part-exchanging their old cars. Try anything to get them through the door. But nothing worked.

That morning, the TV news was filled with images of pubs and restaurants closing down their operations after the previous night's announcement. No one knew how long the shutters would remain down. People looked genuinely terrified. Not just about the virus, but what lay in store for their businesses. How were they going to survive? At that point, there had been no real talk of government help or support. They were all staring into the abyss, financially.

My heart went out to them. What if I'd stayed on at The Crown? What would I have done to make ends meet? How would I have paid the ongoing costs of keeping the place in mothballs? The electric, gas, business rates. And what would I have done with all that stock, the beer especially. It would all be ruined, fit for nothing more than being poured down the drains. I shuddered to think and thanked my lucky stars – again – that I'd made the decision I had.

During my lunch break, I fired off a few texts and emails to people I knew in the licensed trade. It was quite a tight-knit community, the landlords and licensees of Darwen. So I contacted Maxine, the land-lady at The Old Function Room pub where I took part in the quiz each week. Dropped an email to Louise at The Greenfield and to Leon, who ran the Level One nightclub in town, who I knew well. They'd been appreciative. Hearing from them made me realise once more that I'd dodged a bullet. I really had. But I wasn't going to gloat or make light of what was happening. I just extended my sympathies and let them know that I was around if I could help in any way.

As I thought about them, I began also to think about the regulars we'd got to know so well at The Crown. The single guys – and girls – who would come in for a quiet pint and a chat. The friends who would meet up once a week to share each other's troubles or just blow off steam. And then, inevitably, I thought about all the quiz teams. All the players for whom Thursday nights had become such an important escape, a safe haven from the woes of the world. What were they all going to do now?

It was then that an idea began to formulate in my head. What if I ran a quiz online? Just a small one, to keep people in touch and entertained?

It percolated away for a little while. My mind is often prone to flights of fancy but this time I put my overactive imagination on ice. I didn't have the tech skills to pull off anything complicated. If I was going to do it, I'd simply try to replicate my regular Thursday night quiz. Keep it simple. A few rounds of straightforward questions and answers. Maybe on themes like sport or music or geography. Getting everyone together was the most important thing.

I opened up my laptop and hummed and hawed a little. What should I do? Write a group email? Stick it on WhatsApp? I opened up my Facebook page, not something I did very often – I wasn't particularly active on social media. I knew that you could create 'events' there. I looked around and saw the buttons. Without even really thinking about it, I clicked and opened up a blank page. I tapped in a headline: Quiz on Thursday? I then tapped out a note.

'As we can't go out on Thursday to the quiz, I'm thinking of doing one online for everyone? Not sure how I'll do it at the moment, but thought it might be good to have a laugh and give us something to look forward to? Let me know if you are up for it, and feel free to invite other quiz teams or people up for a laugh?'

I didn't have many friends on Facebook. It was mainly confined to my quiz team mates and a few others in the motor and pub trade locally in Darwen. I did a quick tally. I reckoned I'd invited about forty people, max.

I finished setting up the event, clicking on the button that said the post should be confined to 'friends only'. That might include my mum and my brother down in London, but it wasn't going to inter- est them. I then hit 'post', closed down my laptop and forgot about it. A couple of us at the showroom had ordered lunch from a local takeaway. Ordinarily, we'd be rushed off our feet and have little time for anything more than a sandwich. Today was different. We could have had a five-course tasting menu – with wine – and still had time to spare.

By the time we shut up the showroom late that afternoon, I'd forgotten all about the Facebook page. As I drove back to Darwen, I honestly didn't give it a single thought. I was more concerned that Sarah and Jack were OK. And that we had something in the fridge for our Saturday night dinner.

★

Since that day, I've often sat down and tried to imagine what I'd unintentionally set in motion. I've pictured that post of mine as if it was happening in a movie. I've conjured up an image of an elec- trical charge flying down a cable and then into a spaghetti bowl of wiring and onwards. Off out into cyberspace or the internet or whatever you want to call it. Into a million phones, laptops, desktops and devices from Sydney to San Francisco, Hong Kong to Helsinki. I've imagined the faces of people sitting, bored or mindlessly trawling through their social media, then spotting my notice and going 'ah, that's a good idea'. Or 'X would like that, I'll share with them'. And so the event would have been shared by someone else who'd share it with someone else. And on and on – and on. A chain reaction. A viral reaction. (It was only later that the irony of that hit me.) At the time, however, I didn't give this a moment's thought. For the first thirty-six hours after I put the post up on Facebook, I remained blissfully ignorant.

★

Sunday turned out to be a busy day at work. The dealership had got hold of a rare, much-sought-after four-by-four, a Suzuki Jimny. There was normally a scramble when one appeared on the forecourt. They were rarer than hen's teeth. We had a waiting list of people who wanted one. No one was going to turn up to look at it today, so I hit the phones.

I was much more effective as a face-to-face salesman. I could get people to trust me in those conditions. On the phone, it was a different story.

Once again, I found people hesitant. 'Not at the moment.' 'What would I do with it?' But eventually I found a guy who was interested. It wasn't the easiest of sales. We spent the best part of an hour discussing the COVID situation. I could feel him chopping and changing his mind as we spoke. Should I, shouldn't I?

Eventually, I managed to persuade him to put down a deposit on the vehicle. I reassured him that the car would be his no matter what happened in the coming days and weeks. 'It'll be here waiting for you.'

Ian was pleased with me and I left the showroom to head home around five o'clock feeling upbeat, despite the gathering storm clouds. I'd completely forgotten about the quiz. I cooked us dinner, then spent the night half watching TV and half scrolling through news websites on my phone. They were full of speculation about schools and businesses being closed. Of everyone being told to work from home and to stop socialising. But there was nothing concrete. Sarah and I assumed it would be business as usual the next day so had an early night.

*

By Monday, the speculation was at fever pitch. Some big changes were coming. Schools would be closed. People would be ordered to stay at home. It didn't bear thinking about.

Sarah knew it wouldn't impact her. She'd still need to go into her clinic. I wasn't quite sure how it was going to affect the motor trade. People would still need cars, wouldn't they? Maybe not? I really didn't know. Ian hadn't told me otherwise.

I went to work as normal on Monday morning. I was due a day off the following day, Tuesday, anyway, having worked the weekend.

The roads were busy with cars on the school run, as usual. It didn't feel like we were on the edge of something serious happening. My main focus was trying to sell another car to boost my commission. I was going to need it. My hopes were soon dashed.

I'd barely arrived inside the showroom when Ian beckoned me into his office. He'd had a tip-off from head office that we would have to lock up the showroom that night. So we'd been told to get all our ducks in a row. We had quite a lot of work to do.

Once more, it was a non-event of a day from a sales point of view. We didn't have a single customer. For some reason unknown to me, we'd been told to change the point-of-sale material on display on the forecourt, so I spent the morning doing that.

Talk about rearranging the deckchairs on the *Titanic*. I really couldn't see the point of the exercise.

It was close to lunchtime when I noticed a 'ping' on my phone. It was a notification message. Someone wanted to send me a message on Facebook Messenger.

It was a middle-aged lady. I didn't recognise the face. I'd always been very cautious about social media so checked the person out before accepting the message request. They looked legit. Not like one of those obviously fake accounts you avoid like the plague. Her message simply read: 'Can you tell me more about the quiz you are running on Thursday night?'

For a moment, I was at a loss. Thursday night? Then I remembered that I'd set up the event. But how come this person knew about it?

I flipped open my laptop. I'd not even looked at my Facebook page since Saturday. I'm not sure what I was expecting to find, but it certainly wasn't the sight that greeted me when I clicked on the Events page I'd set up.

'What the hell?'

I couldn't believe it. There were seven hundred people 'interested'.

Seven hundred. It was supposed to be forty people in Darwen.

I started looking at the people who'd registered that 'interest'. I recognised one or two, but most were strangers. They were in Manchester and London as well as Darwen.

I sat there for a moment, dumbstruck. Shaking my head and flicking around the page to see if there was any explanation. I looked at the privacy settings. I was sure I'd hit 'friends only' rather than 'public'. But it looked as if it had gone out publicly. The whole world could see it. And that world had started sharing it.

Ian came in for a lunchtime coffee. I must have been in a state of semi-shock because he looked at me strangely.

'You OK? Bad news?'

I showed him the Facebook page and he just whistled.

'Bloody hell.'

The TV news was on. The Prime Minister was making another televised announcement tonight. The chances of us avoiding a total lockdown seemed to be fading by the minute.

'You'll have a damn sight more than seven hundred people by the end of tonight,' Ian said, nodding at the screen. 'Everyone's going to be bored stiff by Thursday.'

I looked at the Facebook page and shook my head again.

'I've got more than that already.'

In the time it had taken him to make a cup of coffee, it had gone up to eight hundred.

I spent that afternoon in a bit of a daze. There was so much going on. The impending lockdown. Shutting down the showroom. And now – to my amazement – this quiz.

I put my laptop away after lunch and left it in my rucksack. I was tempted to pop back and check the number a couple of times, but I had too much to do. I was desperate to try and make one or two more sales before the showroom closed, not that there was much chance of that. But I had to try. I needed the money.

It was only as we finally drew down the shutters and locked up just after five o'clock that I took another look at my laptop.

That familiar shocked feeling returned.

The number of people 'interested' in the event was well into four figures now.

Ian was almost as intrigued as me. When I showed him the ticking number counter, he shook his head.

'I reckon that will be at two thousand by the time you get home.'

I headed home in the evening traffic, a million thoughts flying around. I was concerned about the announcement. What would it mean to us in practical terms? How would it work? Would Sarah and I carry on doing our jobs? And what about Jack and his nursery? There were so many unknowns. But I was also beginning to grow anxious about this quiz. What had I unwittingly unleashed? Was I going to regret it?

Back home, I switched on my desktop computer then opened my Facebook page. I slumped back into my chair. Ian had been right. The number of people who had registered an interest was now well past two thousand.

'What on earth have I done?' I said to myself.

It was fast becoming the most surreal day of my life. I tried to inject a dose of reality by getting on with my normal routine. Sarah had popped across the road to see her mum. She was naturally concerned about how she was coping. I wasn't going to add to Sarah's worries by telling her what had happened on Facebook. Instead, I gave Jack a bath and sorted out dinner. While I rustled up a meal, I put the TV on in the kitchen. As Sarah, Paige and I ate, we were apprehensive. Thankfully, we had Jack to distract us. He was blissfully oblivious to what was going on.

Sarah had made sure her mum was well stocked with food and all she needed if we were to be confined to our homes. Paige wasn't on the best of terms with her family, but she had been in touch too. There was a weird, end-of-days feel to the world. Everyone seemed to be getting ready to batten down the hatches. We really were entering uncharted waters. Not even my dear old grandparents had gone through something like this, and they'd lived in London during the Blitz.

The announcement wasn't due until a little before 9 p.m., so as we waited I looked at the Facebook page once more. I opened it up gingerly. By now, I was almost afraid at what I'd discover.

The number counter was spinning round like a Vegas slot machine in hyperdrive. Two thousand had become four thousand had become six thousand. There were comments piling up as well now. 'Just what I needed.' 'Thanks for doing this. I'm missing my normal quiz night.' It was all positive, but I couldn't really see it with a clear eye. My head was spinning. I was beginning to panic and see the negative side. How was I going to manage this? Did I really want to make myself known to thousands of strangers?

Sarah, Paige and I gathered around the TV just before 9 p.m., Paige and I on the sofa and Sarah in her favourite armchair. The Prime Minister's speech was pretty sombre. The ten-minute announcement was filled with phrases that – we didn't realise – would become ingrained in us over the coming weeks and months.

'Now is the time for everyone to stop non-essential contact and to stop all non-essential travel.' 'We must stay at home.' 'We must protect the NHS and save lives.' The upshot of it all was that everyone was now expected to remain within their homes unless they had an important reason not to do so. Any gathering of more than two people who weren't part of the same household was banned. All social events, whether it was weddings or baptisms, were also off limits. Funerals could still take place, but with only a small number of people attending – and all of them at safe distances. All non-essential travel was also banned, including any visits to friends or family. The police were being given powers to enforce the rules by breaking up gatherings and even issuing fines. The Prime Minister must have known it was terrifying a lot of people, so he tried to sweeten the pill with promises that we would 'beat the coronavirus' and that it may be as little as three weeks until we were freed again. I didn't believe that for a moment. We were in this for the long haul.

As we sat and took stock of what we'd just heard, we looked in detail at the new rules and regulations. As far as I was concerned, I was going to be able to leave the house each day so that I could drive Sarah to work. She was a vulnerable person as well as an essential worker. I had to protect her as best I could. But Paige and I were otherwise confined to barracks. Apart from taking Jack for a brief walk to the park, or queuing to get into the supermarket, I was going to be housebound. The thought filled me with dread. I wasn't great at being cooped up. I knew it was going to be tough for Paige too. She was just twenty-five. She'd lost her father a few years earlier and didn't have a great relationship with her mother. I recognised what she was going through. She felt bad about having landed on our doorstep at the precise moment the world was locked down, but she needn't have. Aside from anything else, she had immediately hit it off with Jack. He loved her. So I assured her she'd be helpful if Sarah or I came under pressure for whatever reason. As it turned out, she'd be busier than either of us could have imagined.

After the drama of the announcement we sat up late, drinking tea in the kitchen. I'd not yet told Sarah about the Facebook quiz page. With so much going on, I'd been in two minds about burdening her with it. Compared to what she was having to deal with, my situation just seemed trivial. Not worth bothering about. Especially since it was all self-inflicted. There was no one to blame for it but me.

I knew I couldn't keep it a secret for long, so I eventually summoned up the strength to tell her.

'There's something you should see, Sarah,' I said sheepishly.

Her reaction was typical. We'd faced a few problems over the years, but we'd dealt with them together. That was how our relationship worked. We just got on with life. Got on with whatever it was that needed facing. Together.

So I could probably have predicted her reaction. Sarah isn't afraid to say what she thinks, and she told me that it seemed like a pretty idiotic thing to have done. Why hadn't I kept the page private? Hadn't it been obvious that loads of people would sign up, given what was going on? But overall, she just thought it was funny. She couldn't help laughing at the sheer number of people who'd now signed up. When I told her how anxious I was about it, she just shrugged and smiled.

'You'll be fine. Just pretend you're in The Crown on a Thursday night. Everyone loved what you did there. Even when you cocked things up.'

Paige was supportive too. She said she'd help me in any way she could. She was far more techie than me, so that was a consolation. They'd told me just what I needed to hear. And it put my mind at rest, for a little while at least. Until I went to bed that night.

As soon as the lights were out and I was alone in the dark, my mind began to run away with itself. It's my curse and it kicked in with a vengeance that night.

I was soon catastrophising, conjuring up all the worst possible scenarios. All the ways in which this could be a complete and utter disaster. 'My quiz style is unique, I get things wrong, I give away answers, I don't take myself seriously. I don't look like a TV presenter. How on earth am I going to run a quiz for twenty thousand people?'

I told myself off a few times. 'Jay. Put this in perspective. Haven't you got bigger things to worry about? As of tomorrow, you and your family are going to be locked in your home while a killer virus runs riot across the country.'

It was true, of course. Millions of people were lying awake in bed that night, tossing and turning, fretting over what lay ahead. We were all dealing with something new, something unprecedented.

Couples were trying to work out how they were going to cope financially and emotionally. How they were going to keep their children safe and sane. We knew people who would wake up in the morning having to look after three kids in two-bedroomed flats in tower blocks. They had no gardens, no balconies, no open spaces to get away from each other. And then there were the elderly and sickly. And those who were already isolated. Their loneliness was only going to deepen. In comparison, my issue wasn't even an issue. It was silly really. And I knew it. But it didn't really help. I just couldn't shake it from my mind.

I slept really badly. I got up a couple of times just to interrupt my train of thought. But when your mind is locked into that kind of downward spiral, it's really hard to break out of it. So it was a relief when the first sliver of morning light began to appear on the hills to the east of Darwen. I hadn't properly worked out my next steps, but I had, at least, decided on two things I was definitely *not* going to do.

At one point during that long, restless night, I wondered whether I should tell people it was a joke.

'Yes, that's it,' I told myself. 'I'll tell everyone that I was kidding. I wasn't really going to run a quiz. It was just me being Jay. Being an idiot.'

That idea didn't last long. I'd always worried that people thought me stupid. That wouldn't reflect well on me at all. People really would think I'd been an idiot, and I didn't want that.

More importantly, I'd rejected the darkest and most worrying thought. It hadn't lingered long, but it had hung there long enough to stir up some memories and images from my past. I'd managed to dispatch it before it took root.

'No, Jay,' I'd scolded myself. 'You don't run away from it all. Not any more.'

ROUND TWO

4

THE WRITING'S ON THE WALL

In which direction do birds fly in winter?
Jay's Virtual Pub Quiz No 4, April 2020

Late one afternoon in April 2003, a few days after my twenty-first birthday, I boarded a train at Victoria station bound for the coastal port of Dover in Kent. The carriages were dotted with commuters and families who had been up in London for the day, but also people weighed down with rucksacks and holdalls heading for the ferries leaving that evening to cross the Channel to France.

I found a space in an almost empty carriage, as far away from the rest of the passengers as possible. I didn't want to be around other people and, given the way I looked and was behaving, people probably didn't want to be around me either. I was dressed pretty scruffily in jeans and a jacket and carrying a small rucksack and a carrier bag full of tins of beer. I was in a pretty agitated state, which was hardly surprising.

It may sound strange, but the decision to take my own life had been a snap one. I'd only decided earlier that day.

Once I'd made my mind up, though, I had been pretty calm and methodical. To begin with, at least. I'd gathered up the only valuable possessions I had – an Xbox and some video games – and headed to an exchange shop in central London. I'd got £75 or so, enough for a train ticket, some beers and half a dozen packets of paracetamol. I knew there were legal limits to how many I could buy in one shop so had visited three different pharmacies and bought the maximum two packets allowable at each one. I'd then popped into a cheap off-licence near Victoria station and bought a dozen tins of Foster's lager.

My plan had its own, seemingly rational, logic. I'd take an overdose while I was on the train. If it worked, I'd be dead by the time I reached the coast. If not, I had a Plan B. I was going to head from Dover to Beachy Head, the notorious beauty spot, where I would jump five hundred feet off the cliffs.

As the train got underway and the carriage rattled along through the suburbs of south London, I swallowed a fistful of pills, swilling them down with a few cans of beer. My mind was soon a half-drunk fog, filled, as usual, with random and often conflicting thoughts but even more mixed up and paranoid than usual. Part of me was obsessively trying to gauge if the tablets were working. It was hard to tell, my mind was racing so fast. Another part of me was planning what was to come if and when I got to Dover. How would I get to Beachy Head? Bus? Hitch a lift? Walk? I was in a manic state, my brain was jumping around, flashing up fragments of memories. Painful and difficult ones. From my recent as well as my more distant past. From the events that had persuaded me to listen to the little voice that had taken over in my head. The one saying: 'I might as well leave because no one will miss me.'

★

It had, by now, been more than four years since I'd lost my grandad. It hadn't taken long for the loss to unmoor me. Without the one great guardrail and stabilising influence I'd had in my life, my mental health had started collapsing steadily.

The downward slide had begun with a setback at work. As I approached my eighteenth birthday, things had been going really well. I'd put in the hours and grafted hard at the McDonald's in Wimbledon. I'd started earning enough money to rent my own flat. I felt liberated. I'd not been happy living with my mum and Simon, my sister and Conor. Now I had money in my pocket, a purpose in life. I was on my way. I felt like I was growing up. Becoming an adult. Or, at least, that's what I'd persuaded myself.

My immediate bosses at McDonald's had been really happy with my progress and I'd been due for a promotion to assistant manager. It had been presented almost as a *fait accompli*. It was in the bag. But shortly before my birthday, the company's senior management told me it wasn't going to be possible. I was still too young. I'd not reacted well.

It was the sort of upset most people go through, especially when they're at the start of their working life, as I was. But looking back at it now, I can see that I was so desperate for approval and acknowledgement that I couldn't cope when things went in the opposite direction. I had become hypersensitive to rejection of any kind. I was finding it harder and harder to handle. In this case, it was exacerbated by the huge trust issues I had and connected, I was sure, to what had happened with the family friend – something I'd still not mentioned to a soul since it happened.

So I took the management's decision really badly. I felt it was a slap in the face. It was another example of people not being truthful. Exploiting me.

I'd quit, and not politely. I'd just told them to shove their job. Preferably where the sun didn't tend to shine.

It was a silly move. But the impulsiveness I'd begun to show as a youngster had got worse. I was doing things without thinking through the consequences. With my grandad gone, there was no one to rein me in and keep me grounded.

I wasn't out of work for long. Over the next year or so I had a succession of jobs, from bar work to working in a children's theatre. But nothing lasted. I got bored or cheesed off with my co-workers all too easily. It was more to do with me than them. I was deeply insecure and vulnerable. And none of this was helped by the appearance in my life of a figure I'd never expected to meet. My father.

My mother was the one who instigated it. Out of the blue, she'd sat me down for a chat one evening. 'Would you like to meet your father?' she'd asked. 'He wants to meet you.' It had taken me a while to absorb it and at first I was reluctant. I didn't feel I owed him anything. He'd been an anonymous figure up till now. Why did he deserve it? And what was I going to gain from it? I was still missing my grandad badly and it would only remind me of my loss. He'd never live up to him, I was certain of it. But in the end, curiosity had got the better of me. I'd thought: *Why not? What harm can it do?* I clearly wasn't thinking very straight.

Given what I'd been told when I was younger, I had a vague notion that my father was some kind of tough guy. I had a memory of someone in the family calling him 'a nasty piece of work'. Despite its genteel image, Wimbledon had its share of hard nuts, mainly skinheads and thugs that used to be associated with the football terraces when I was younger. I didn't spend much time picturing what he looked like, but on the rare occasions I did, I imagined he was one of those. A bit of a hooligan. But when I arrived at the pub in Wimbledon that night, I had no real idea what to expect.

If it had been a Hollywood movie, of course, it would have been a dramatic moment accompanied by even more dramatic music. We'd have seen each other and fallen into each other's arms. Or started wary of each other but grown to make a connection. But truth be told, it was a crashing anticlimax.

He did manage to live up to one of my expectations. He had short – almost skinhead-style – hair and tattoos. It turned out he was a Chelsea fan, while by now I was an avid Spurs fan. Chelsea and their fans had a bad reputation, they were beyond the pale, and I'm afraid I was quick to cast my father to type.

It was a meeting between two complete strangers, and a very odd experience. I knew nothing about him and vice versa. He told me he was a refuse collector – a dustbin man – working for an inner-city borough council. But the more he told me about himself and his life, the more I realised that I didn't care. We had no common ground, and I sensed he was discovering that too.

Despite his absence in my life these past eighteen years, he claimed to have been taking an interest in me from afar. A close relative of his lived in the same neighbourhood as my mum and had occasionally spoken to her, he reckoned. He'd had a child at the same junior school as me. He mentioned the fact I'd been on TV but clearly knew little about the details.

He had about him a kind of bravado, I suppose you could call it. I felt like he was talking at me rather than to me. At one point he was implying that he'd made sure I was looked after in the pubs and bars of Wimbledon. He seemed to be saying that he knew all the bouncers and bar staff in the area and had told them to keep an eye out for me. He didn't know that I didn't really go to nightclubs and didn't need anyone to 'watch out for me'. All I was doing was having an occasional drink with friends, singing karaoke and entering local pub quizzes. Hardly a risk to life and limb.

It struck me that he was 'bigging himself up', making himself appear like he was a figure of influence, not just in my life but in the wider world.

There wasn't really a balloon to be deflated, but if there had been it just quietly lost air as the evening progressed.

By the end of the evening, I got the impression that he was as disappointed in me as I was in him. I don't think he could understand much about me – least of all why I would support Spurs over Chelsea, as he quizzed me on it several times.

We stayed in touch, and I met him on three or four occasions at most. But we quickly lost interest. After that, I was aware of his presence around Wimbledon but didn't really engage. Other people might have been eager to continue, to ask more questions. Who was he and why hadn't he been a part of my upbringing? There was no question that I had a hole in my life. I'd lost my father figure. My emotional support. But my real father wasn't what I needed. Or, at least, that's what I felt. All those questions: Why had he left me?

Why had he not been in contact when I was growing up? They weren't important to me. As far as I was concerned, it was water under the bridge. The damage had been done and nothing was going to compensate for it.

Of course, I can see now that I was still repressing stuff. Protecting myself from being hurt again. Not that I managed that entirely. Having my father in my life was unsettling and uncomfortable. I was even less sure who the hell I was. I wanted to push away any thought that I was his son. I dreaded the idea that anyone thought me a chip off the old block. Outwardly, I was quite gregarious. But I was becoming more and more inward-looking emotionally. I was also growing more and more insecure and unhappy. I felt like my life was going nowhere. I was constantly taking one step forward, two steps back. Being in and out of work meant that I couldn't afford to continue renting my own flat, so I had to move back in with my mum, Conor and my sister (my mum had divorced Simon by now). But rather than going back into my old bedroom, I was demoted to the smaller bedroom that had previously been Conor's. That summed up my situation perfectly. Stifled. I was effectively living back under her rules. Having to account for myself and my movements. Like a teenager again.

Conor and I got on well. I think he looked up to me as a big brother figure. I knew my mum valued that. I provided Conor with a male presence that was missing otherwise. But it wasn't the life I wanted long term.

My real beacon of light during that time was the social life I had carved out in Wimbledon. I had a small group of friends with whom I went to pub quizzes and karaoke nights. The quizzes were probably my way of saying I wasn't as stupid as my school grades suggested. That there was a brain inside my head. Karaoke tapped into the frustrated actor within. I'd done it for a while. I'd had some singing lessons when I was acting and had learned how to control my breathing. I always got a good reaction when I sang. One or two friends had suggested I take it further, but I'd never had the courage to sing without the words in front of me and a noisy, largely distracted crowd chatting away while I did my thing. It was an escape more than anything else.

I'd struck up a romance too. Her name was Zoe and we'd been part of a group of friends at first. We both enjoyed karaoke and had begun singing duets together. We belted out ballads like 'Written in the Stars' by Elton John and LeAnn Rimes and 'We've Got Tonight' by Ronan Keating and Lulu. We'd sometimes go out and sing three or four nights a week. As far as I was concerned, we were a couple. Boyfriend and girlfriend. We were together for around nine months. I definitely wanted it to become more serious, but when I eventually summoned the courage to tell her, she basically ended it. She said she just wanted us to remain friends. We did, to an extent. But it was another rejection and inside I was devastated.

I was no Adonis, I knew. I didn't feel like an attractive person. And I began asking myself whether another woman would ever come along.

I was in a terrible state, dealing with a new sensation – a broken heart. Outwardly, I may have appeared confident, but that was the actor in me. Inwardly, this only added to everything I was already deeply insecure about – my looks, my everything. I felt unattractive, unloved, unwanted.

When it comes to your mental health, it is a litany of things that drag you down. But then it only takes one of those things to snap you. Breaking up with Zoe was the tipping point.

It took time for it to coalesce, for all the forces to come together. But when they did, it happened suddenly. It wasn't self-pitying, or at least I didn't see it that way. I wasn't looking for sympathy. I was becoming too self-sufficient for that. To me, it was just a fact. I was surplus to requirements. I'd tried to carve out a place for myself in the world, but there wasn't one available. I was a square peg in a round hole. I'd tried. I always tried. But it hadn't worked. I can still remember the thought forming in my head. 'No one would miss me if I took myself away.'

Which was how I found myself on that train to Dover.

*

The eerie calm I'd shown when I first made the decision had faded as the day went on. As I'd become more frazzled and manic, my plan had begun to unravel into an amateurish mess.

I'd actually intended heading to Eastbourne, which was nearer to Beachy Head. But in my chaotic state I'd got on a train to Dover instead. As if that wasn't bad enough, I'd miscalculated on the pills as well. The truth was that an overdose of paracetamol would have severely or fatally damaged my liver but it wouldn't have killed me instantly. It would take a few days and maybe even then it mightn't succeed. I'd also failed to account for the fact that the human body is a resourceful machine and reacts when it's under attack. I'd not eaten much that day, for obvious reasons. So a fistful of tablets mixed with fizzy lager had produced a fairly swift reaction. I'd had to hide away in the train toilet, vomiting. My body was doing what it had to do and trying to expel it all.

By the time I reached Canterbury, two-thirds of the way to Dover from London, I was feeling so awful I decided to get off the train. I needed to be sick again. Then I wanted somewhere to curl up and sleep.

I was completely disoriented by now, so I wandered off into the streets. I must have been a terrible sight. I was delirious, barely able to walk straight and covered in puke. It was a cold evening and the cobbled back streets of the old part of Canterbury were empty. But even if they hadn't been, I'm sure people would have crossed the road to avoid me.

I managed to pull myself together enough to look for a sign for a hospital or a police station or somewhere, but there was nothing. But then I saw a phone box – I didn't have a mobile phone – so I went in and dialled 999. Just as I'd done when I was a nine-year-old running away a dozen years earlier. Was it a cry for help again? Perhaps. If it was, that help duly arrived in the shape of an ambulance.

I must have passed out at some point because my next memory is of waking up in a hospital bed with doctors and nurses circling around me.

The medical professionals were great, as were the referral workers who appeared the next morning. They were very supportive, empathetic. I gave them my name and age, but when they asked for an address I said I didn't have one, which was how I felt at that point. I gave the same answer when I was asked about my next of kin. I didn't have one, I didn't have a home. I remained in the hospital for a day or so, during which time a few more people came to talk to me. Two were from a local mental health charity. They were very professional. Again, they were very supportive. One of them said he didn't believe I had really meant to harm myself. Deep down, I wasn't so sure. I could still feel an urge to end things. That voice was still telling me that no one would miss me. The fact I was here in a strange town, surrounded by strangers, only underlined that feeling. But I'd suppressed all those thoughts while I remained in hospital. In truth, I just needed to recover and to sleep.

After a couple more days I was taken to a hostel in Gillingham on the Medway Estuary in Kent, about twenty miles from Canterbury. It was run by the charity who had come to see me and was a kind of halfway house to help people with mental health issues. I'd been officially designated as homeless by now as well. It was a fairly nondescript building in a quiet part of the town, which suited me perfectly. Nondescript and quiet was just what I needed. I had my own, very simple room, with a bed, a sink and a table. I spent the first day or so in there, mostly sleeping as I continued to recover.

After a few days I ventured out from the hostel and wandered around Gillingham, but I kept myself to myself. I didn't engage with anyone. It was the same in the hostel. My trust issues were still a major obstacle. It wasn't just that I didn't believe in asking for help, I'd now got to the point where I didn't believe people when they did offer assistance. I thought there was a hidden agenda. Even here, in a town far from home where there was no reason to suspect anyone of an ulterior motive. I was developing a form of paranoia.

Outwardly, however, I projected an image of being on the mend. My acting came in handy there. I knew how to mask the real me. Project a different persona. At one point, it was suggested that I start taking some medication, some antidepressants. I batted away the idea with a smile and a 'No, no, no. I'm fine, honestly'. But the truth was, I was still having suicidal thoughts. While out walking, I'd found a bridge that ran over an old disused railway line. I'd cross over it every day. I would look down on the overgrown tracks forty or so feet below and think to myself that it could be my final resting place. I could throw myself off. But then the constant internal struggle would begin. Endless questions. What if the fall didn't kill me? It was an isolated place. What if I lay there for days, weeks, months, dying a slow, agonising death? That, ultimately, was the only thing that stopped me.

None of this was the fault of the people at the hostel. They really were the consummate professionals. One key worker in particular tried her best to bring me out of my shell. She talked to me most days. I engaged to an extent. I told her the bare bones of my situation, but barely scratched the surface in terms of the real issues and events that had driven me to this point. It was silly of me, really. I desperately needed some counselling, someone to open me up. But my feelings were buried too deep and without the trust, no one could excavate them.

The chats were helpful in restoring some normality though. After a few weeks, I began to come out of my room into the communal TV area. I didn't talk to any of the other residents. They were pretty self-contained too. They were dealing with their own issues, I could tell. But I did begin to appreciate being among people, back in the world again. On my own terms, obviously.

I remained in the hostel for almost two months, during which time I began to feel steadily better. More positive. The suicidal thoughts abated. I knew I'd need to look for a new job soon and was coming round to the idea of remaining in this area. It was far enough from London to allow me to be anonymous. I could start afresh. No one knew anything about me, and I had no intention of contacting anyone who did, especially my mum or my sister. I needed a break from them. I needed to be able to set the clock to zero. It didn't occur to me that they might be worried out of their minds. I was just too lost in my own head to think of anyone except myself.

In the short term, I took advantage of the benefits system, which covered the costs of my hostel while I looked for something more permanent that I'd pay for myself. I used the small amount of money I had left over to buy some clothes from charity shops. I'd arrived at the hostel with nothing but the clothes on my back and had been wearing hand-me-downs for the past month or so.

The most tangible sign that I was returning to my old self came when I went out one night to a local pub in Gillingham. I'd noticed the pub's karaoke night advertised a few times walking around town, but I'd not been able to summon the courage to go. That night, I felt right and headed off. The pub was quite busy and for a moment I thought about turning round and heading straight back to the hostel. But the atmosphere was really friendly, and as the karaoke got going it began to feel even more welcoming. People were being kind and supportive to everyone who got up and sang.

I'd always seen it as an escape, a way to let go of all my emotions and pretend to be someone else. That's exactly how I approached it here. No one knew who I was anyway, but I could now pretend to be someone completely different. So I put my name down to sing a song I liked by Craig David featuring Sting called 'Rise and Fall'. The song had a line about when you're about to give up and 'it seems as though the writing's on the wall', which seemed to sum up the way I'd felt a few weeks earlier.

It went down really well – I got a rapturous round of applause, and people came up to me to say well done.

I didn't hang around for long afterwards. I had a drink then headed back to the hostel. I didn't want to engage any further with people. But lying awake in bed that night, I felt more positive than I had for weeks. The evening had reminded me that there was some life in me. I wasn't as dead inside as I had begun to feel. But I knew too that it was a small step, and nothing more than that.

I hadn't really addressed my problems. Nothing had changed in that respect. The demons that had driven me on to that train to Dover months earlier were still there. I thought back to the words in that song I'd sung tonight. For me, the writing was still on the wall. And the fight was far from over. It had hardly begun.

5

THE ACCIDENTAL QUIZMASTER

What does the A stand for in FAQ?
Jay's Virtual Pub Quiz No 7, April 2020

What does the B stand for in USB?
Jay's Virtual Pub Quiz Book 2

What does TT stand for in Isle of Man TT racing?
Jay's Virtual Pub Quiz No 27, June 2020

On Tuesday 24 March 2020, we all woke up to the grim new reality. We were in lockdown.

It was a really weird feeling, looking out at the deserted neighbourhood that morning. Ours is normally a fairly busy street first thing, but there wasn't a soul to be seen. As Sarah, Jack, Paige and I had our breakfast, we had the BBC News on the TV. Unsurprisingly, it was completely dominated by this new state of emergency and how it was going to work. We did our best to explain it to Jack, but he was too young to really take anything in. As far as he was concerned, it must have seemed like a huge bonus. He would have a house full of adults to play with most of the time.

At least we did have a house full of people to interact with each other. As I listened to the news, I was already thinking about the damage lockdown was going to do to people, especially those who were isolated and alone. No one seemed to be giving them much thought.

Sarah and I hadn't really prepared for weeks of confinement. We hadn't been hoarding and stockpiling toilet rolls and tins of baked beans. We'd both been too busy getting on with our lives. So after dropping Sarah off at the clinic where she worked, my first task was to head to a supermarket and stock the house up. I went to the nearest big store and saw an enormous queue, snaking its way around the car park. There must have been close to a hundred people there, waiting impatiently in line. They were only letting a few people in at a time.

I joined the queue, slipping on one of the face masks that Sarah had brought home from the clinic. It felt odd, but I suspected I'd have to get used to it.

A lot of those in the queue looked anxious. One woman flinched and covered herself up with her scarf whenever she heard someone cough. Another couple were worrying about whether the shelves inside had been restocked. Apparently, the place had been stripped bare the previous night. Several gave up and left the queue, muttering to themselves.

If this was the new normal, I didn't like it much.

I'd brought my phone with me so at least I could monitor things while I waited to see if there were any bananas and baked beans left inside.

The activity on my Facebook page only added to my feeling that we'd all entered some kind of alternative universe. Or two universes, in my case. The disconnect between the real world and what was happening online was ridiculous. I still had to pinch myself at the numbers. They had continued to climb overnight. It was now well over forty thousand people. I had a swathe of new messages from people as far away as Cyprus, New York and New Zealand. They all wanted to know more detail about what was happening on Thursday night. The where, when and how.

If only I had the answer. I replied to as many as I could, but simply couldn't keep up with it. I felt bad, but knew the best thing I could do was to get it all sorted and then post something online with the details. Whatever they might be.

I had never been a great one for accepting other people's help. But one of the many lessons I'd learned from my past was that sometimes you need to. No matter how suspicious and paranoid you might be at the time. My experience in Kent after my overdose attempt sprang briefly into my mind. Back then, I'd been unwilling to give anyone the benefit of the doubt. I had trusted no one. And been a fool for doing so. I was older and a little wiser now, so I was determined to at least try to take people up on offers.

I knew that compiling the quiz would be the easy bit. I'd been doing that for years. I had a big archive with thousands of questions that I could dip into. I'd put them all on a USB stick as a back-up. All I had to do was remember where I'd put it. I'd then construct five rounds of ten questions. I'd decided that was the format I'd use. Fifty questions, five rounds. I'd make the categories straightforward – start with Science and Nature then follow with TV and Film, Music, a History round and then a General Knowledge round to conclude. I'd briefly wondered whether I needed to make the questions more international in flavour. But I'd decided against it. For a start, I wasn't convinced that anyone beyond my regulars from Darwen was actually going to show up. But also, the vast majority of people who'd expressed an interest were from the UK. Last but not least, most of the questions in my files were general and answerable by anyone. OK, there were a few music and TV questions that someone in Dallas or Dubai might scratch their heads at, but that was a risk I'd have to take. My big dilemma was still where and how to do it?

Facebook was the obvious place, given that I'd started it there. But I wasn't technically savvy enough to set it all up. Things hadn't exactly gone to plan when I'd set the event up the previous Saturday. I didn't want to make another mistake.

It was here that Paige came to the rescue. She was grateful for the distraction. She was, a little like me, not someone who could sit around doing nothing all day. I called on one or two other friends as well, especially ones who were comfortable doing techie stuff.

My questions had been the same to everyone.

What are people expecting? If it's some kind of super slick quiz with graphics and fancy music and an app, then they were going to be sorely disappointed. That was a non-starter.

After chatting to Paige and emailing a couple of mates, I decided it couldn't be the kind of competitive quiz I'd run in a pub. People would basically have to scribble down their answers on paper. It would then be up to them to declare their scores. There was no way I could collate, mark and rank them all. As one friend, Brent, jokingly said to me: 'What are you going to do? Go through them in reverse order? And in twenty thousand and thirteenth place is . . .'

People would have to organise that themselves. Within COVID rules wherever they were in the world.

'It has to be just for fun. Friends and families can play against each other. That's the best I can do,' I told Paige as we sat down over the umpteenth cup of tea. She agreed.

By Tuesday night, the number of people interested on the Facebook page had gone through six figures. There were more than one hundred thousand people lined up to play. The clock was ticking. I now had forty-eight hours to organise a quiz for them. It was terrifying, but also, I had to admit, exhilarating at the same time. The good news, I told myself, was that if I ignored the Facebook page, I would have plenty of peace and quiet to get on with it. After all, there was nothing else going on in the world, was there? They turned out to be famous last words.

*

It was a little after supper that an email popped up from a journalist from an online magazine called WhyNow. 'Wonder if you're free to do an interview about your quiz?' At first, I thought it was a wind-up, a prank by an old regular from The Crown. But when I looked closer, it was legit. I replied, and before I knew it I was on the phone talking to someone.

I'd be asked the same question countless times again in the coming days and weeks. But first time out, it just felt bizarre, like an out-of-body experience. I was talking publicly about something that had, until now, largely lived inside my overactive imagination.

'So why did you set up the quiz?'

'Well, umm, I thought it would be a bit of fun for my mates.'

'And how did so many people get to know about it? Didn't you mark it private on Facebook?'

'I thought I had, but obviously I made a mistake. Or there's been an accident.'

That, of course, gave them the headline they wanted. Soon, there was an article online: The Accidental Quizmaster. I didn't mind. It was true. Despite many attempts to explain how it had happened, no one really knew. Including Facebook themselves. I'd sent them a message and got nothing more than a standard 'we'll get back to you' answer.

By the end of the night I'd had more interview requests, including from the Associated Press. I wasn't an expert when it came to the media, but I knew that was significant. It was an international news agency and it would syndicate the story absolutely everywhere. I braced myself for another spike in the numbers on Facebook.

I left my phone downstairs when I went to bed that night. I had to be up early for Jack again in the morning. If I kept it by my bedside, I wouldn't get a wink of sleep.

★

By Wednesday, the trickle of interview requests had become a torrent. That seems to be the way it works with news stories. And how some go viral, while others fade away into the memory. It's a domino effect. Sometimes, the first domino misses the second one and that's that. At other times, the first collides with the second, which hits the third and on it goes. That's what happened with me. Thanks to the Associated Press story and others, the dominoes were soon falling in what seemed like an endless chain reaction. I spoke to one of my local papers, the *Lancashire Telegraph*, and a handful of radio stations, including Heart FM, Smooth and Capital FM.

I was then contacted by BBC Lancashire, which got Sarah and her family really excited. It was what a lot of them listened to routinely. Sarah's phone was buzzing with messages when they heard me. By this point, I had more than 400,000 people interested on Facebook. They must have recognised the anxiety in my voice. Where was it going to end? Was I going to end up with egg on my face?

By that lunchtime, I'd had other approaches as well. Some were just a nuisance. A bunch of online marketers and advertising companies contacted me via Facebook. They were all offering ad campaigns and marketing advice – for a hefty fee, obviously. I just ignored them. I didn't really need anyone to 'boost' interest. Quite the opposite. If someone had contacted me asking if they could slow things down, I might have been willing to have a conversation.

A couple of other emails had been from people planning to run rival online quizzes. One was a bit unpleasant. He claimed he'd set up his quiz before me and that I should basically be redirecting all my audience to his event. I took a look at his page on Facebook and saw that he had fewer than two dozen followers. I sent him a polite note and wished him luck. It seemed more and more like pure fluke that I had the numbers I had.

The other quizmasters and mistresses I heard from were much less aggressive and simply wondered whether I could help them acquire more players. But the most intriguing email that day came from a guy who'd appeared on a very popular TV reality show. He was a really entrepreneurial character. A Londoner like me, with a touch of the East End barrow boy about him. I had a vague memory of seeing him on the series. He had set up some kind of online quiz platform several months earlier. I looked it up. It was quite slick but clearly didn't have many users. Certainly not as many as were lined up to join mine.

I agreed to have a chat with him on a video conference platform that Paige had introduced me to. It was called Zoom. It was odd talking to complete strangers on my desktop.

The guy was very enthusiastic. I could see how he'd got on TV. His pitch to me was pretty straightforward: this could be good for us both. He had the platform, I had the audience. A rather big one. If we combined the two, we could achieve a lot.

It all sounded quite sensible. And appealing. But the minute he started talking about money, I knew it wasn't going to work.

His idea was to charge people maybe two, three or even five pounds to compete. And we could do it weekly or even twice weekly during lockdown. There would be production costs, but whatever profit was left at the end would be divided up between us. He wasn't specific about who took what share. All he kept saying was that I should 'do the maths'. 'Four hundred thousand people at five pounds a pop.'

It set alarm bells off in a couple of ways. Firstly, this was simply something I'd done for fun. To entertain some friends. And as far as I was concerned, that's what it had to remain. It was also a one-off. It wasn't something I was planning on repeating. The past few days had been mind-bending enough. Having to do this more than once didn't bear thinking about. At that point, I wanted it out of the way so that I could get on with the rest of my life. Apart from anything else, I needed to talk to Ian about my position at work. He'd sent me a note saying that the showroom was staying closed, for now at least.

Despite that, I also knew that I couldn't – or more to the point, shouldn't – charge for my quiz. Shutting out people now wouldn't reflect well on me. If it was a 'paid-for' quiz, I should have declared that at the beginning. And besides, four hundred thousand people weren't going to pay five pounds to play a quiz run by some bloke in Darwen.

I said I'd bear in mind what he'd proposed and talk to him again. After I'd got Thursday night's quiz out of the way. He seemed a little put out and I didn't blame him for trying to get in on the opportunity. But by the time we ended the call, I was pretty certain I wouldn't be calling him back on it.

By Wednesday night, I was growing exhausted by it all. But I knew I still had to get the technicalities right. It was Paige who suggested that I run the quiz on YouTube. The moment she said it, I realised it made sense. It was, after all, the world's biggest video hosting site. And millions of people ran livestreams there all the time.

I dived in and got a page set up fairly quickly. I needed to come up with a name. I experimented with a few variations. But in the end I decided – again – to make my life simple. Why overcomplicate what was already turning into an overly complicated situation? So I came up with something that did what it said on the tin. It was my normal Thursday night pub quiz, held virtually and hosted by me. Jay. I pressed the 'save' button and watched the wheel whirl around on my computer. I got the confirmation through on an email and opened the newly created page. There it was: Jay's Virtual Pub Quiz. I was in business.

I decided to try it out by posting a message to everyone who'd expressed an interest. I simply couldn't keep up with the messages and requests for clarification on Facebook. For every one query I answered, I'd get three new ones. I was like King Canute, trying in vain to stem the tide.

I had a shave and put on a clean hoodie, and recorded it just before 8 p.m. that night. Almost exactly twenty-four hours before I was due to go live the following night, Thursday.

It was only a four-minute message, but it gave me an opportunity to try out the system I'd be using. To get some confidence too. I didn't want to suffer silly, self-inflicted tech issues in front of hundreds of thousands of people. Fail to prepare, prepare to fail, and all that.

I'd set up my computer downstairs on the table in our living room. It took me a couple of attempts to get the lighting and the camera angle right. I wasn't close enough to the camera at first. I was probably subconsciously shying away from it. But I eventually got it all worked out.

I'd made the background deliberately bare. I might add something on Thursday night but, for now, it seemed the right approach. It wasn't that I was afraid of giving away my address. Even the criminals were stuck indoors at the moment. It was more that I wanted to retain some kind of privacy. I definitely didn't want people looking at family photos of me, Sarah and Jack.

I hit the button on YouTube and started recording. I introduced myself and thanked everyone for their interest. I then laid out the plan for the following night.

A lady had started a nationwide campaign to clap for the NHS workers and carers at 8 p.m. every Thursday, which clashed directly with the time I'd chosen. The clapping idea was catching on fast, quite rightly. Sarah and her mum and relatives were all planning on doing it. I couldn't possibly try to undermine something so important. So I decided that I'd start at 7.45 p.m., do an introduction, and then let everyone pop out for a few minutes at 8 p.m. to give the NHS the support it thoroughly deserved.

I felt I had to explain the situation on scoring the quiz. I said the numbers were simply too vast to be able to announce any kind of winner. But I promised to give shout-outs to as many teams as possible if they tallied up their totals and sent them in at the end. I certainly intended to mention anyone who got fifty out of fifty questions right.

I'd seen that people were organising Skype, Facebook and FaceTime parties. I encouraged them to run competitions between each other. I couldn't stop myself from warning, as I always did at my pub quizzes, against using Google or other search engines to find answers. It just wasn't in the spirit of things, basically.

I ended by raising something that had been percolating in my mind all day. Ever since I'd started talking to the press, in fact. Almost everyone had asked me whether this was a one-off. At first, I'd said yes. Which was true. Until now, I'd just wanted to get it out of the way. To clear the decks. But the momentum had become so strong, I'd begun to wonder. What if? I was genuinely worried whether Ian was going to be able to justify keeping me on the payroll while the show-room was closed. What was I going to do for money? Maybe, just maybe, the quiz might keep me going somehow? Not in the way the TV entrepreneur had suggested, but in some other, more modest way I hadn't yet worked out. So I concluded by saying that if Thursday night was a success and people wanted to carry on, then I was more than happy to do so. 'I've got nothing else to do,' I said.

I was encouraged by the number of people who sent messages after I'd posted. They were almost universally positive, a mirror of the kind comments I'd been getting on Facebook for days now.

I tried to spend the rest of the night away from the quiz. I read Jack a bedtime story, then sat watching TV with Sarah and Paige. We watched a little bit of the news, which, naturally, was almost one hundred per cent about COVID and lockdown. The number of people dying was slowly ticking up. Sarah said the number of cases locally was very low at the moment, but it seemed inevitable that the virus would arrive in Darwen. It was when, not if. The news that most interested me that night was about the plan that the Chancellor of the Exchequer was apparently putting together to help businesses survive. I'd had a note that evening from Ian at the show-room. Because I'd only just started work, he wasn't sure where I stood. He'd promised to get back to me as soon as he could. I knew everyone was operating in the dark, so I wasn't surprised. The furlough scheme, as it was being called, might be just what he – and I – needed to keep afloat.

My phone was busy with messages from friends around town. Most wanted to know about the quiz, but some were just chats about how we were all faring. We were forty-eight hours into lock-down. That time had flown by for me. It had seemed like two hours. But some of my friends weren't finding it so easy. A couple said they'd got through those first fraught nights with a few too many beers or glasses of wine. So far, I'd resisted pretty well. And I decided to do the same tonight. For a start, Jack was an early riser and I liked to be up with him to give him breakfast. But I also needed to have a clear head the following day. It was Thursday. The day of the quiz. Tempting though it was after the day I'd had, I was going to resist.

But then I made a schoolboy error. As I got ready to go up to bed, I took one last look at the Facebook page. I couldn't believe my eyes. I now had close to half a million people interested. I then compounded the mistake by looking at the YouTube channel. Thousands of people had viewed my little video. Scrolling down the page, I saw that hundreds of them had left messages. Friends, families, boyfriends and girlfriends, regular quiz teams, random strangers. They were still there now, posting notes, plastering the page with smiley-face and thumbs-up emojis. I read a few. 'Such a great idea! We're forming a team in Geneva, Switzerland, competing against family in Manchester and York. Appreciate your efforts.' 'Buzzing for this looking forward to it. Got a team together. Great idea bringing some normality to us all in these crazy times :)' 'Haha sorry for being one of the ones who has infiltrated your little town's quiz. But . . . congrats on going viral with such a good idea. I have a team of three excited to take part and we can't wait to join you tomorrow night.' It would have taken half the night to read them all.

I was gobsmacked. I could only assume it was the publicity. More and more people were latching on to it – and no longer just on Facebook.

The quiz was already viral. Was it possible to go mega-viral? To do what Kim Kardashian threatened and break the internet? If so, I must now be in danger of doing that. Something had kicked in somewhere, I had no idea what. But it seemed like half the Western world – and a chunk of the rest – was ready and waiting. Waiting for me to ask fifty random questions from my living room!

How I managed to climb the stairs and put my head down on the pillow without having a very stiff whisky, I still don't know.

6

TIGGER

In which book was Christopher Robin a character?
Kids' Quiz 2 in Jay's Virtual Pub Quiz Book 2

For a time, during my early twenties, my nickname was Tigger. I used to count it as a compliment. To me, it meant people thought I was energetic, enthusiastic – fun. They liked me. Let's face it, who didn't love Tigger.

It was a few years ago, when I was reading the Winnie the Pooh books with my son, Jack, that it struck me how apt the comparison really was. And wasn't, at the same time.

Pooh's creator, A.A. Milne, wrote that Tigger 'always seems bigger because of his bounces'. It was probably why I got the nickname. At that time in my life, I was trying to pick myself up. To bounce back. In doing so, I wanted to appear stronger. I did it by being a live wire. A Duracell bunny, as someone else called me. Behind the mask, though, I wasn't very much like Tigger at all. 'Tiggers never get lost,' Milne wrote. I was still a long way off the right path. Nowhere near it, in fact.

It wasn't for want of trying. And for a while, as I continued my recovery down in Kent, I felt like I'd found my way. With the help of the charity whose hostel had looked after me, I managed to get myself a little flat in the port town of Rochester. I made one or two friends. Built a bit of a social life. The ghosts of the recent past weren't totally exorcised, but I felt like I'd started to inch my way back into the world.

I liked the Medway towns. Rochester and adjoining Chatham were an antidote to London. Smaller, friendlier, cheaper too. I hadn't found a job so was still on benefits and didn't have much money.

I desperately wanted to rid myself of that feeling that there wasn't a place for me in the world. I wanted to be a round peg in the round-shaped world. And for a couple of months, at least, I'd begun to make a decent fist of it. The fact that no one knew me helped, of course. No one had prejudged or formed any kind of opinion about me. People took me at face value.

It was a sign of how comfortable I was that three months or so after I'd left London, I decided to make contact with some old friends back in Wimbledon. I went into a local library and opened up an old email account. I hadn't looked at it since I'd headed off for Dover, weeks earlier. As I scrolled through, I found an email from an address I didn't recognise.

The sender was asking if I was OK. But then they mentioned that they were still drinking at the same pub I'd always go to on a Friday night, The Corner Pin next to Wimbledon greyhound track, near Plough Lane. 'Might see you there one Friday?' they wrote.

It caught me off-guard. I wasn't sure which of my friends it was, but they clearly knew me and my habits well. I didn't respond immediately, but after some time I wrote back.

'I'll let you know when I'm coming. It'll be good to see the old gang.'

I wasn't sure if I was ready for it. Going back to London was a big step. I'd stuck to my guns and made no contact with my mum or family. Should I tell them I was heading back? I didn't feel inclined to. They were, as far as I was concerned, the root of all my problems.

I mulled it over for a while and, on at least one occasion, went to the railway station ready to head into London, but backed off before buying a ticket. Eventually, however, I summoned up the strength.

It was a mistake. What I hadn't realised was that the emails were coming from my aunt, my mother's sister. She was basically phishing. The upshot of it was that when I turned up at the pub, there was a reception committee waiting for me. I walked in to be greeted by, of all people, my father. 'Where the hell have you been? Your mother has been worried sick about you,' he told me.

I tried to explain.

'I needed to get away,' I told him. 'I needed a break from her. From everything back here.'

'But you could have told her you were alive,' he said. 'She thought you were dead.'

It was selfish of me, I know. I'm a parent myself now and I can't imagine how I'd feel if Jack disappeared. But that was part of my illness then. It's what happens when you are in a deep depression – you are lost within your own problems, locked in within your own head. Inside that head, my mother, my father and the neighbourhood where I'd grown up were all part of a problem I was still failing to solve.

My father took me to see my mother that night and we spent a few pretty intense hours talking. She, understandably, vented her anger on me. She couldn't understand why the authorities hadn't told her I'd been admitted to hospital. 'Why weren't your next of kin told?' She was furious when I told her that I'd denied even having any. Just as baffling to her was the fact that I'd allowed myself to be registered as homeless. 'You've got a home,' she said. Looking back on it, it wasn't my finest hour. No mother, no matter how bad the relationship, should hear that her son has denied he had a home. In effect, I'd also denied she existed.

I did my best to explain my choices. That night I'd landed in Canterbury, my mental state was all over the place and I really hadn't thought anything through, I told her. I wasn't capable.

She was hurt and baffled, and I couldn't blame her for that. How was she – how was anyone – going to follow the thought processes that went on in my head that day? We talked a bit more. We weren't the greatest of communicators, but we tried to reach some kind of understanding. We agreed that I'd go back to Rochester and carry on my life there. Try to make a go of it. But I agreed to stay in touch, if only to let her know that I was still in one piece. I owed her that much, I conceded.

*

I've often thought about it. I think I'd have remained in Kent if I hadn't gone to Wimbledon that night. I was becoming so settled that I'd have carved out some kind of a life for myself in Rochester. Found a job, fitted in. But, as it turned out, I was slowly drawn back to London.

I'd recovered some self-confidence and landed a good job as a salesman with a mobile phone company, Carphone Warehouse. I was going to be working at their stores across Greater London. Before that, I would do my training in Acton, west London. I asked to be posted to the nearest outlet to Rochester, which was in Orpington in Kent. I could commute there from Rochester. But instead they posted me to Clapham, in south-west London. It was simply too far – and too expensive – for me to travel back and forth every day.

So, reluctantly, I'd gone back to live with my mother. Natalie had left home by now, so it was just her, me and Conor, who was now ten or so. I settled back into a routine of sorts. On a couple of occasions, when my mum was away, I looked after Conor on my own. I got him up and off to school each morning, then cooked his meals when he got home. We bumped along together perfectly well. We became close.

My job was demanding and I built a social life around it, so my mum and I weren't under each other's feet too much. It allowed us to keep the peace. A part of her, I'm sure, was glad to have me home, not least so that there was a male adult presence in the house for Conor again. But it was like walking on eggshells at times. We rubbed each other up the wrong way too easily.

I spent even less time at home when I began a new relationship. Her name was Christina. She lived near us with her family. I'd met her through her brother Paul, who was part of my social circle. She was a few years younger than me, but we hit it off. We shared a love of football. She'd grown up in Somerset, where her dad still lived after separating from her mum, and supported Yeovil Town.

Our romance blossomed pretty quickly. I couldn't have been happier. Relationships weren't easy for me, but I felt my confidence and trust beginning to return.

It was a measure of how settled I was at that point that I'd become a part-time quizmaster. It was at a pub called the William Morris, overlooking the River Wandle, not far from where my mum and Christina's family lived. I only did it a handful of times because the elderly landlord couldn't be bothered with it. But I enjoyed the challenge of coming up with interesting questions that kept the audience engaged. I even got used to sometimes rowdy interaction with the audience. That and my nights singing karaoke were probably the closest thing to therapy I've ever had. I genuinely loved those evenings; they took me away from my struggles. And they all helped the rehabilitation that was, I felt, slowly gathering strength.

We'd been together for a few months when Christina and I were faced with a big decision. Her stepdad was in the army and had been posted away from London to Catterick barracks, near Darlington up in Yorkshire. Her mother and two brothers were going with him. Christina was in a dilemma: whether to go with them or not. It was made more difficult by the fact that we were now engaged. I'd bought her a ring and had even gone down to Somerset to do the traditional thing of asking her father for his daughter's hand in marriage. We had no plans for a wedding at that point, but we did want to move in together.

It wasn't an easy choice. Christina was a family-oriented person. She was very close to her mum. The idea of being alone in London scared her a little. I was reluctant to relocate to the north, so I asked my mum if Christina could move in with us. I thought she'd feel happier in a family environment, even if it was a fairly unstable one. My mum agreed, a little reluctantly.

It didn't take long for us to fall out. It wasn't necessarily my mum's fault. We were young and had different habits to her. The flare-ups were over the littlest things: shoes being left out, washing-up not being done. The sort of domestic disputes that happen in every home. But it was enough for me to start looking around for somewhere else to live. We eventually found a lovely little two-bedroomed house; we moved in and were very happy there. I even quit Carphone Warehouse and took a job working near Christina in Waterloo. We commuted in and out of work together each day.

It worked well for almost a year, but Christina missed her mum badly and travelled back and forth to Yorkshire a lot. So when the annual lease on our house came up for renewal, we bit the bullet and decided to move to Darlington together. It wasn't a tough call for me. I wanted to be with Christina, and relations with my mum and the rest of my family had never been exactly rosy. By the time we were ready to head off, I felt even more that way.

*

My mother and I had always had a spiky relationship. We seemed to have a particular gift for winding each other up. We were probably too similar. Both sensitive. Both too quick to feel slighted. And then both too prone to say things that were hard to take back. I suspect lots of parents and siblings have that kind of relationship. We just took it a bit too far at times, I guess.

She didn't think it was a good idea for me to leave London and head way up to Darlington – in her words, 'chasing a woman'. I was pursuing something that wouldn't work. 'It'll end in tears.' As far as she was concerned, I was selfish and just running away again. I was undeterred. It only proved to me why I needed to get away again.

Christina headed up to Yorkshire a couple of days ahead of me while I cleared out the house and handed back the keys. My mother appeared on the final day. It was obvious straight away that she was spoiling for a fight.

I still had a set of keys for her house and was going to drop them off. But she'd already decided I'd forgotten all about it and was going to take them up to Darlington.

'Typical. Selfish as ever,' she said. 'You never think of this family. Only yourself.'

Something inside me just snapped.

'How can you call me selfish when for years I've kept a secret to protect this family? I've kept quiet about something that could have torn this family apart.'

'What are you talking about now?' she said.

Maybe it was bravado on my part because I knew I was leaving. Or maybe I just felt that I couldn't continue to carry the burden any longer. I told her exactly what had happened when I was left with the family friend that weekend all those years ago. I didn't go into graphic detail. It was difficult enough opening up that steel-shuttered compartment in my mind.

My mother just sat there. Stunned – briefly – into silence. When she eventually reacted, I was shocked by her response.

Her exact words were: 'Nonsense. Lies. I don't believe you. Prove it.'

I was transported back to my childhood. To the times when, if I complained or caused trouble, the reaction had always been: 'Jay's acting up again.' I was someone who overdramatised. Overplayed things. I wasn't to be believed. But I wasn't a child any more. And I wasn't going to take it.

I let rip and told her everything. How it had contributed to the breakdown that had almost led me to take my life. How it had forced me away from London – and her. The conversation had come a dozen years too late. It had been festering inside me all that time, so now that it was finally coming out, it did so in a fury. I channelled all the anger and resentment I'd felt, rightly or wrongly, towards my mother for allowing me to be put in such a vulnerable position at that age. Of course, the whole family was at fault. But as far as I was concerned, she was the focus of my anger. She should have known. She should have protected me. For me, it was a release of emotions that had been bottled up for far too long. It was cathartic. It was the beginning of some kind of closure. As it turned out, in more ways than one.

Throughout the time I was talking, my mum was just shaking her head. She kept saying, 'Lies, all lies. Where is all this coming from? You're making this up.' I just carried on. I wasn't going to be shouted down. Eventually, she just walked away, waving her arms at me as she went.

With my mother and I, it was always about who had the last word. On this occasion, it went to her. She stopped and turned.

'If you're going, get gone,' she said with one final dismissive wave.

And so that's what I did. I left. I got gone.

I felt a mixture of relief and sadness as I travelled north the next day. I'd finally tackled something I should have broached a long time ago. A huge weight had lifted off my shoulders. The hurtful part was that, to my mind at least, my mother had sided with my abuser rather than me. But if that was the way it was going to be, then so be it.

It was a seismic moment between us. Afterwards, the rift between my mum and me felt unbridgeable. We didn't speak again for eleven years.

*

Leaving London felt like an escape and Christina's family welcomed me with open arms. I landed a job working for a kitchen- and bathroom-fitting company. For a few months, all was set fair.

It wasn't a perfect set-up in Darlington. Down in London, we'd had a small house to ourselves. We'd made it our home, our little sanctuary. We did what we wanted, ate what we wanted, watched what we wanted on TV. Up in Darlington, we had a small bedroom in a house we shared with four other people – Christina's mum and stepdad, and her two brothers. I got along well enough with them all, but I quickly began to feel we were too much on top of each other. We didn't feel like we had any privacy.

The natural thing to do would have been to get our own place. But by the time we were ready to do that, things were already unravelling. The giddy excitement of our engagement, and all the plans we'd shared back then, had given way to a dawning reality. We both had boring jobs and lived in a frankly overcrowded house in a pretty unexciting town.

The final straw came when a friend hinted that there was something going on between Christina and her boss at the DIY warehouse where she worked. She denied it, but of course the damage was done. She accused me of not trusting her, which was true.

Despite our age, we handled it fairly maturely. We both agreed that it wasn't going to work out. The odds were stacked against us. I decided to leave the north-east and head back down to London.

I blamed myself, naturally. I'd failed. When we got engaged, we both imagined a future with children and a nice house and all the clichéd trappings of a happy marriage. But we were young and naive. Yes, I was only twenty-four, but it was clear already that I wasn't going to be earning big bucks and providing us with a five-star lifestyle. The insecurities I felt about being a bad fiancé had soon begun to blend in with the ones I'd always felt about myself. I wasn't attractive. I wasn't marriage material. I was too fragile emotionally. Too much of a mess, basically. All those familiar, destructive thoughts whirred through my mind again.

★

I arrived back in London knowing it was now a city where my options were growing more and more limited.

Going back to my mum was not on the cards, clearly. We'd not exchanged a word since our bust-up about her friend. And I was too ashamed to tell her what a failure my move to Darlington had been. My pride, my ego, my self-confidence were all on life support. I didn't need her to switch it off completely with an 'I told you so'.

Instead, I turned to my network of friends for help. Thankfully, I still had some.

The company I'd worked with up in Darlington had offered me work in their depot in Redhill, in Surrey. Beggars couldn't be choosers. I accepted the transfer. I didn't know anyone in the town and couldn't afford to stay there, so I took up an invitation to stay with a friend, Jen. She was a single mum and lived in a tiny flat in Mitcham with her months-old baby. I slept on her sofa and would get up at 5 a.m. to get to work for 7 a.m. But Jen was having problems with her baby and would be up all night trying to settle the child. That meant I couldn't get access to the sofa until at least midnight, sometimes later. It wasn't ideal. Unsurprisingly, I couldn't always get to work on time. It wasn't long before I was handed my notice.

I fell back on bar work and landed a regular job in a pub in Morden. It was an environment in which I was comfortable. I liked the atmosphere, the buzz, the camaraderie of a pub. I responded well to it.

That's when I picked up my nickname. Tigger. Outwardly, I was trying to convince everyone, not least myself, that I was all right, but I was just overcompensating massively. Inside, I'd been reduced to rubble again. It wouldn't have taken a professional psychologist to work out where I was headed.

The one miracle in all this was that I didn't turn to drink or drugs to deal with my troubles. And for that I thanked my grandad.

I thought about him often. It's silly, I know, but there were times when I sensed his spirit nearby. While my grandma loved her whisky, my grandad was almost teetotal. He used to drink Kaliber, the alcohol-free lager. He had told me that I had to be careful with alcohol. 'It can get the better of a person,' he said sagely. I don't know if he'd had a drink problem in the past or had someone close to him suffer from alcoholism, but I never saw him drink heavily.

I'd spent a lot of time drinking in – and working in – pubs over the years. I'd get drunk occasionally, but I'd only ever lost control of myself twice. Once was after a night out with some friends, when I got carried away and climbed on a parapet inside a multistorey car park. It looked like the prow of a ship, so I climbed up to mimic Leonardo DiCaprio in *Titanic* by screaming 'I'm the King of the World'. Quite how I arrived at that conclusion, I've never quite worked out. I wasn't the king of anything.

The other was on the eve of a big induction day at my new employers Carphone Warehouse, when I went out in Croydon with an old friend. He insisted we do shots and we drank a ridiculous amount. I headed home to catch the tram back to Morden, where I was living, and basically walked into a closed door, injuring my head and passing out in the process. I woke up in a hospital and made the induction the following day by the skin of my teeth. My fellow inductees thought I was some sort of class clown, arriving with a great big lump on my head. I'd not got really drunk since.

It was one of the few silver linings during that period. If I'd succumbed to drink at that point, that really would have been the end of me.

The final downward spiral was predictable. Ask anyone who works with homeless people and they'll have seen and heard it a thousand times. It was a slow-motion train wreck. And it all happened in the late spring and early summer of 2007.

It began, as before, when I lost my job. It wasn't my fault – the pub I was working in closed down. I didn't have any money so I began to sofa surf, sleeping wherever I could with whichever friend happened to have any spare space. My final stop-off was a friend who lived in Morden. Back on my old patch, no more than half a mile from where my mother lived. I dreaded bumping into her, or indeed anyone else I knew. For a few weeks I was holed up in this house, claiming benefits, afraid to go out too much in case I bumped into the wrong person. I had too much time to think. Too much time living inside my head. It was again inevitable: the demons returned with a vengeance.

One night, I slipped out of my friend's house in the middle of the night and walked the three miles back to where I'd grown up with my grandparents in Wimbledon Park. I wandered past my child-hood home and places from my school days. That familiar thought had returned: *No one's going to miss me.*

I headed to a railway bridge across the busy main line that passed through Wimbledon from Surrey into Waterloo. I was going to throw myself off into the path of a speeding train. There were plenty of them. But, again, my mind began working in the most bizarre way. The logical side of my brain began to ask if it was fair on the person who would find me on the railway tracks in the morning. That one unselfish thought saved me and I abandoned the plan, ringing the Samaritans instead from a phone box.

This time, the person on the other end of the call must have been really alarmed by my mental state because they called the police, who quickly arrived on the scene and found me wandering the street near the phone box. They took me into the station, where I was assessed by someone. I didn't know what I wanted at that precise moment, but the one thing I did know was that I didn't want to go back into the 'system'. To be institutionalised or stuck in a vanilla room in a hostel. That would just have been a repeat of what I now regarded as the same useless routine. So once more I went into denial mode. Actor mode. After a few hours, the police were persuaded that I wasn't really suicidal and let me walk out the door.

It was history repeating itself. I was on a loop, behaving the same way as I'd done when I was a child and when I was twenty-one. I was locked into the same spiral that I'd experienced before. I had to break it. I had to do something drastic. And so I did. It all seemed so logical at the time.

I was staying at a friend's flat and waited a few days until I got a benefit cheque. I cashed it in and left. I didn't say anything. I didn't take much with me, just a rucksack with a few clothes. I spent the next fortnight or so living and sleeping in parks and on night Tubes and buses. With just £70 in my pocket, I was soon learning how to make it last by picking up discarded travel tickets and takeaways.

There was a rhythm and – strangely – a purpose to what I was doing. It was about surviving from each day to the next. In a way, I was pitting my wits against the world. A world where nothing was predictable. Where I knew there was danger, potentially, around every corner. Looking back on it, I can see it was reckless, but at the time I was up for the challenge.

I was sitting on a bus one afternoon, heading east through Kensington and Knightsbridge towards the West End, when I had a sudden light-bulb moment. I saw the future with complete clarity. *This is your life now*, I said to myself. *You don't live in a house; you live outside. So let's go and find somewhere to settle.*

I hopped off the bus at Trafalgar Square and dived into a camping store off the Strand, where I bought a cheap sleeping bag with my last £11. It was June and the sun was shining, so I decided to walk around the city that night scouting for my new base. My new 'home'.

I knew I didn't want to hang out where all the other rough sleepers congregated. The Strand and Covent Garden, in particular, had dozens, if not hundreds, of people curled up in doorways, under arches or near hot-air vents. Along Tottenham Court Road and Oxford Street too, there were places where the pavements outside major stores were lined with pop-up tents and cardboard constructions housing the homeless.

I wasn't afraid of my fellow street dweller. It wasn't that. I'd simply decided that I didn't want to be a part of 'society', or whatever you want to call it, any more. I had removed myself. I wasn't looking for companionship or safety in numbers. I wasn't looking for places where the many charities circulated offering hot drinks and food and access to shelters. Quite the opposite. I wanted to stay off their radar. I'd been there before. I wanted to do it differently this time. See what it was like to fly solo. Just rely on myself.

I had scoped out one possible location. It was a rotunda inside Hyde Park, near Speakers' Corner. I'd slept there a couple of times during the day. But it was a non-starter because it was inside the park, one of the so-called Royal Parks. It was illegal to sleep there between 11 p.m. and 5 a.m. I'd be running the risk of being turfed out or, worse, being arrested each night. So I turned my attention towards the River Thames and an area that I'd always loved, the Embankment.

The elegant riverfront runs along the north side of the Thames between the Houses of Parliament and Blackfriars Bridge, and at night in particular, with all of London lit up, it's a breathtaking place. You can sit there, looking south across the river to the London Eye and the South Bank, west to Big Ben and east to St Paul's and the City of London. There's no view like it anywhere in the world. It's also the most peaceful place. It's sometimes hard to believe you're in the heart of one of the planet's busiest cities. And to sit there while the waves of the Thames lap gently against the river wall beneath you is just magical.

I knew there was a long line of ornate benches, raised slightly above the pavement that ran between Hungerford and Waterloo bridges, near Embankment Tube station. I headed there and walked up and down, weighing them up as potential homes. The bench nearest the exit from Embankment station was too exposed. Too many people came in and out of the Tube there. I'd be constantly bothered by drunks and idiots. The ones further along towards Waterloo Bridge were too isolated. Those same drunks and idiots might be tempted to harm me while I was sleeping. I had to be aware of the danger; there was a risk sleeping rough wherever I set myself up. Eventually, I decided I liked the look of the second bench along heading east when you came out of the Tube station.

All the benches along the riverfront had wrought-iron arm rests in the middle, which, in theory, was a deterrent to anyone who might want to sleep there. But I didn't see it being a problem. That night, I gathered my few belongings together and positioned myself with my legs raised over the arm rests, tucked myself up, fully clothed, in my sleeping bag and settled down for the night. It was a warm evening. It was midweek, so there wasn't a soul around. I lay there and looked across the moonlit river, my mind slowing down. *Yes, this is the place,* I told myself. *This is home.*

I decided that home needed a name. In keeping with the British tradition of giving houses on the same side of a street odd and even numbers, I decided that, as the second along, this would be number three. *That's it. Number Three, Riverside View, Victoria Embankment.*

That night, I felt oddly at ease with myself. I felt a certainty, a kind of calm that I'd not had for a long time, perhaps ever. This was where I would now base myself. No 3. It was a risk, of course. It may work, it may not. But something would happen here, of that I was in no doubt. My life would either come to a natural end at this place, or something would occur to change it that would put me finally on the right path. I was at peace with the fact that it would be one or the other. And either was fine.

ROUND THREE

7

ZERO HOUR

In which song did Elton John have his bags
packed, pre-flight at 9 a.m.?
Jay's Virtual Pub Quiz No 1, 26 March 2020

By Thursday 26 March, the third full day of lockdown, most people's lives were slowing to a crawl. Sarah and I had friends, especially those with young children, who were grumbling about the boredom that had already set in and how every minute seemed to last an hour.

My life, by contrast, seemed to have been speeded up, like some old Keystone Cops silent movie. My hours passed in what seemed like seconds, everything a frantic blur. I didn't have enough time to think. I was being carried along towards the start of the quiz at 8 p.m. What I called Zero Hour. There were moments when I had zero confidence that I was going to be able to pull it off.

After a fitful night's sleep, I was up at the crack of dawn as usual to look after Jack. I made him his breakfast while Sarah got ready for work. Driving her to the clinic, Darwen seemed even more of a ghost town than the previous day. The pavements were empty; vans and delivery lorries were few and far between. The one exception was the supermarket. A ragged queue of shoppers was again curled around the car park. I needed a couple of small items but didn't bother joining. The clock was ticking.

The figures on Facebook and YouTube had become almost meaningless by now – a string of zeros. The comments sections were a seemingly endless flurry of messages and emojis. I spotted people as far afield as California and Kenya. I had no idea what time it was going to be there at 8 p.m. tonight. At least I'd got up early enough to do some final prep work. I still had to add finishing touches. Make a couple of decisions.

Paige had a slick new laptop that she'd offered me. I didn't trust my clapped-out old computer, so I'd taken her up on it. I'd also revamped the look of the live feed a wee bit. I'd rewatched the previous night's YouTube video and decided it needed improving, so I experimented again with camera positions in our living room. I'd also had a change of heart and discreetly put a couple of photos on a shelf in the background, including one of my and Sarah's wedding day. Another of me with her and Jack. I was proud of them. Of us. It also made me look like a normal bloke rather than some odd, slightly shifty character who had invaded everyone's living rooms. I'd put a Spurs scarf up for good measure. I knew that would invite a few comments – especially from fans of our arch-rivals in north London, Arsenal – but it was, again, a way of humanising me. Of making me seem exactly what I was, a normal bloke. Well, normal*ish*.

I was probably overanalysing things as usual, but that was me. That was my way.

The good news was that I'd finally settled on fifty questions that I'd extracted from my files. Five rounds – Science and Nature, TV and Film, Music, a History round on 'Name the Year When', and a General Knowledge round to finish.

Throughout, I tried to remember the lessons I'd learned cutting my teeth at The Greenfield and The Crown. I needed to make the quiz an enjoyable experience. I had to keep everyone engaged. Just as I had tried to do during my first two hundred and fifty quizzes. The stakes seemed slightly higher today though. As my email folder was constantly reminding me.

I'd fielded lots more media requests and had done as many interviews as I could. But by midday, the butterflies were building and I found it hard to concentrate on anything. My stomach seemed to be clenching itself up into an ever-tightening knot.

I wasn't helped by the mini crisis that blew up at lunchtime. A message had popped up on Facebook from someone complaining that photos of his young daughter had somehow ended up on the Events page for the quiz. He was furious that we didn't have permission to use them. This, typically, had been blown up by someone else, who suggested the page was some cynical scam designed to 'harvest' photos. It set alarm bells ringing. I was effectively being called 'a dodgy so-and-so'. And probably worse. For a moment, I went into panic mode. The whole thing might fall apart before I even got to Zero Hour. Thankfully, I pulled myself together and with the help of Paige and some other friends I worked out that it was an issue with Facebook. Somehow, it was automatically displaying photographs from the albums of people who signed up to the Events page. It wasn't just adding their profile photos, it was gathering photos of their family and children too. I kept apologising and promising we were on it. That didn't stop a few people making more snide remarks, of course. But by mid-afternoon it was sorted. We'd been on to Facebook and they'd corrected it.

I was learning so much, so fast. But I could have done without the drama.

Sarah finished work early so as to help me out and be by my side. Paige was there too, my tech guru and social media supervisor. I appreciated both their presences. I'd have quietly imploded without them.

By the end of the afternoon, I'd tested and retested the tech a dozen times. I'd printed out the questions. I'd even selected my wardrobe with Sarah: a blue checked shirt. I didn't want to look scruffy or like I didn't care about my appearance in any way, but at the same time I didn't want to look too formal. It wasn't *University Challenge* or *Mastermind*. I'd called it a Virtual Pub Quiz. I wanted it to feel that way. Like a night at one of the thousands of locals up and down the country that weren't able to run their quizzes this week.

We managed to get something to eat around six o'clock. I barely squeezed down more than a few mouthfuls; the nerves were too overpowering.

By seven o'clock I was pacing around the room, reading and rereading the list of questions. A little voice in my head kept nagging away. *Make sure there aren't any silly mistakes. I don't want two hundred thousand people laughing at me.*

It was a bit of a superstition of mine to have a drink at my side when I did a quiz at The Crown and before that at The Greenfield. I'd need one more than ever tonight, so around seven thirty I slipped into the kitchen and made myself a large gin and tonic.

Everything was set for me to go live, as promised, at 7.50 p.m. A little after 7.45 p.m., I scooped up the printouts, plonked my gin and tonic on the table and took a big breath.

'Right, let's do this,' I said.

Jack had gone to bed by now, leaving Sarah free to give me moral support. She sat down with Paige on the sofa, both just off camera. Paige had another laptop, which she was going to use to monitor things. I logged on to the YouTube page. We'd decided that was the best way to run the quiz. The Facebook feed would automatically pick it up at the same time. Paige had checked it out and it was running fine.

I was amazed by the sight that greeted me when the page came up. There were still a few minutes to go until the official start time but there were already five thousand people waiting for me. Five thousand people – five thousand teams – were so eager that they'd turned up early. And that number was rising at lightning speed as more and more people logged on.

'This is nuts,' I said.

A stream of text was already un-scrolling on the live message board at the top right of the screen. People were saying hi, thanking me for doing the quiz or announcing their quiz team names and locations. Among the earliest were the *Quaranteam*, which I thought was clever, and *Two's Company, Three's an Arrest*, which was a bit risqué. It was all very supportive, which was a relief, especially after the scare earlier in the day.

The three seconds or so it took for the page to connect my live feed via the laptop camera seemed to last an eternity. I had visions of it freezing or me losing the internet connection. But then the red button on the screen began flashing. I was live. Zero Hour had finally arrived.

I'd spent most of the last seventy-two hours or so going over and over in my head what I'd do, mentally rehearsing what I'd say, how I'd introduce myself. I had toyed with all sorts of intros. Clever one-liners. Mimics of other famous quiz programmes. But the moment I saw that light come on, my brain froze. I was taken back to my time as a young actor when – on a couple of occasions – I'd gone completely blank on stage. I laughed nervously and gave myself a talking-to. And then I just said the first thing that came into my head.

'Hello, good evening, I just looked at the numbers and I probably shouldn't have done,' I said. 'This is absolutely mental, absolutely crazy. This started as a local quiz and it's suddenly out of nowhere snowballed, I don't even know how it's come to this. I'm sitting down because I'm trying not to shake too much.'

For the next couple of minutes, I ran through the same spiel that I'd gone through the previous evening. But I soon realised that I'd miscalculated. I still had a few minutes to go until the 8 p.m. 'clap for carers', so I tried to improvise. Fill in some time.

By now, the messages were moving so fast, all I could do was register the occasional location. Spain. Namibia. Norwich. Kenya. Crowthorne.

'Oh, Canada,' I said excitedly.

Someone picked up on the Spurs scarf behind me, so I bumbled on about that for a moment. 'I'm a Spurs fan. Even though we're absolutely sh . . .'

I heard Sarah take a sharp intake of breath.

'Shocking.'

Some players were quite emotional. One, a lady called Mary in London, caught my eye in the comments.

Your wife is a wonderful woman and you are a kind soul. I am crying just watching this, and so proud to live in this country. Now let the games begin . . . xxxx

I tried my best to remain coherent but every now and again the scale of the numbers on the screen hit me.

'This is mad, this is the most surreal night of my life,' I said, my brain flooded once more.

And it was true.

When it came to eight o'clock, I stepped out onto the street with Sarah and Paige. It was a relief to be away from the screen for a moment and the blast of early-evening air did me some more good. The street and the estate across from us were dotted with people. Families, couples, people who'd come out on their own. As it struck eight o'clock, they started making a din – cheering, clapping, whistling, banging pots and pans.

'You OK?' Sarah kept asking me.

'Yeah, fine, fine.' It was my old self-defence system. I recognised it.

Sarah's mum had come out from her house across the road and waved at me. I half-crossed the empty street so as to hear her better.

'Everyone's watching,' she shouted.

I gave her a thumbs-up.

I wasn't sure if that made me feel any better at all.

My stomach was still performing somersaults. And with good reason. By the time I got back to the screen, the number of people signed in on YouTube was over eighty thousand. And that wasn't eighty thousand people. That was eighty thousand teams. Some were individuals or couples, but I knew from the comments already that a lot were made up of three, four, five, maybe even more people. I had no idea of the actual number of people watching. It really wasn't something that was healthy for me to think about. I certainly wasn't going to contemplate what was happening over on Facebook, where, I suspected, there were even more.

I waffled on a little bit about how important the clapping was – not just for Sarah and all the others who worked for the NHS, but for friends who worked in the retail sector at supermarkets and running logistics operations.

'They're on their knees too,' I said. 'And they deserve our support.'

But I could see in the comments that people hadn't come for a political statement. I needed to be a place where the c-word wasn't used.

'OK. Let's go,' I said. 'Ladies and gentlemen. My two-hundred-and-fifty-first quiz.'

Sarah punched the air and let out a little 'yay'. She must have been one of the very few people in the world who knew what it meant. As far as I was aware, no one from Canada or Namibia was a regular at The Crown in Darwen.

I'd figured a general science and nature round was a good introduction. So I began there.

'Round one. Question one. What is the largest internal organ in the human body?'

I spotted the problem almost immediately. A stream of answers began sliding down the comments bar in the top right-hand corner of my screen.

Liver. Brain. Liver. Liver. Skin. Heart. Lungs. Liver.

Some people clearly hadn't grasped that they needed to write their answers on a sheet of paper at home. It wasn't an online contest.

'Please don't write the answers in the comments,' I said as politely as I could. 'Even if they're the wrong ones.'

It had little impact, but I couldn't hang around. I pressed on.

'How many wings does a mosquito have?' I said.

The screen was soon flooded with answers again.

Four. Six. None after I've squashed it. Four.

Players were now expressing their frustration with those who were filling up the comments section.

DON'T WRITE IN THE ANSWERS.

It was a problem. And it was clearly spoiling the quiz for some people.

At least the next question was more difficult.

'Approximately what percentage of the Earth's surface is covered by water? Sixty-one per cent, seventy-one per cent or eighty-one per cent?'

It didn't really matter what answers people put on the comments stream. No one was sure of the right one.

As I picked my way through the rest of the first round, I kept fiddling with the screen, trying to work out how to fix this glitch. Paige was doing the same thing on her screen, but it was a couple of the players who came up with the solution. Ironically, they provided the answer in the comments bar. 'I've been told that the best way around this is to go to full-screen mode. That way, you don't see people putting answers on the comments section,' I said, repeating their advice.

I felt bad. I got to the end of the first round thinking I'd already made a howling error. Possibly ruined the quiz before it had even begun. But I was overthinking it as usual. No one really seemed to care. To judge by the majority of the comments, people were having a good time. I had to remind myself that was the main object of the exercise.

Aside from the answers, there were hundreds of other comments. Some were embarrassingly complimentary.

Chris Tarrant eat your heart out . . . a TV career for you.

What's this guy's name? I want to send him some fan mail.

Pub quiz guy should be knighted.

I love you!

Others were funny. One wag said I needed a ladder to straighten out the photos on display behind me. They were pretty lopsided, I had to concede. A couple of others reckoned my scarf was positioned in such a way it made me look like I had a ponytail haircut. Or, as one player put it: *hang dog ears.*

I'd left a plant, some dried reeds, in the background. Even that was fuel for some jokers.

Who's the person sitting on the floor with wild hair?

Mate, your plant has died.

Sarah tried her best to point out anything that caught her eye, but it was a losing battle. There were too many comments flying in. It was the same with the weird and wonderful locations. Rwanda. New Zealand. Argentina. Ukraine. At one point, a message flashed up: *hey from Antarctica.* I really didn't know whether to believe that. What I did know was that they'd probably struggle with the very UK-centric rounds coming up on TV and Film and Music. 'Who won the first ever *Pop Idol*?' wasn't going to mean much to the teams in Australia and certainly not in Argentina. 'How many contestants are on each team in *University Challenge*?' wouldn't ring many bells in Kyiv or Cape Town. But it was too late now. I pressed on. I figured the bulk of my audience was in the UK. And a lot of the overseas players seemed to be ex-pats, Brits living or working overseas.

Throughout all this, I couldn't help noticing the little counter underneath my image ticking relentlessly upwards. By the time I took a break at the end of round three, there were ninety-four thousand teams. Paige said there was a similar number now playing on Facebook. I didn't even want to attempt the maths. But I sensed that could mean I had an audience of well over half a million people.

I stepped away from the screen and slipped into the kitchen for a break and to fix myself a second gin and tonic. It was giving me the Dutch courage I needed. It was numbing my nerves too.

I pressed on with the second half of the quiz, rounds four and five. Each round was taking me ten minutes or so. The whole quiz was going to run for ninety minutes or more unless I speeded up. But no one seemed to mind. To judge from the comments, a lot of people were treating the event as a social get-together, albeit a virtual one. And they seemed to be enjoying a drink – like me.

More red wine please.

Going for a large voddie.

Is there a toilet in this pub?

You always look for the bad rather than the good, I suppose. So while the stream of comments was ninety-nine per cent positive, I, of course, was drawn to the negatives ones. And as the night wore on and some people got a little worse for wear, one or two unpleasant comments began to creep in. I noticed a couple.

Need a bit more charisma.

NONCE.

Another player kept making bizarre comments about Rose West, the wife of the notorious serial killer Fred West. I didn't know whether that was some kind of slur on my appearance or an obscure joke. No one else seemed to understand it either, and – to my relief – several players told whoever was behind the comments in no uncertain terms to go forth and multiply.

All dodgy comments are being reported to YouTube. No haters here.

I had been braced for the rival quizmaster I'd encountered earlier in the week to pop up to challenge one of my answers or just generally make trouble. But I saw no sign of him. He may have been overwhelmed by the wave of positive energy and comment. I hoped so.

By the time I hit the home straight and the final round on general knowledge, I could feel the weight lifting off my shoulders.

Again, there were some questions that were very much geared to a UK audience. 'Which UK football club remains the only side to win the FA Cup while being a non-league side?' 'Gavin and Stacey was set in Essex and which Welsh town?' But it no longer mattered. The finishing line was in sight.

I'd chosen the fiftieth and final question deliberately. Not because I was feeling cocky or confident but merely because during the week running up to tonight, I'd looked it up out of curiosity.

'The current world record for an online quiz according to the *Guinness World Records* books stands at 16, 162 or 1,622 people?'

As I looked at the counter on YouTube alone, we were way, way ahead of that. The players had spotted this too.

You've broken it.

You've smashed it.

Give Guinness a call.

We're all record breakers.

As far as I was concerned, we'd definitely beaten it, but I said I doubted that Guinness World Records would officially recognise it.

'Unless someone watching works for them,' I added, only half joking. For now, at least, it wasn't a huge concern.

I spent the final section of the evening reading out the answers. But I could feel the weight of the world leaving me. I was nearly there.

People were soon sending in their scores. Some had done well, others not so much. I couldn't stop myself saying 'oh bless' when someone said they'd got three questions right out of fifty. Another guy had seemingly done even worse. *I did not get any questions right have I won a prize?*

Some friends sent in their scores too. One – Geoff, a regular at The Crown – got twenty-five right. He would have been on his own competing. It meant a lot to me to know I'd been able to break the boredom of his new lockdown routine for an hour or so. Scores came in from around the world. The family from Rwanda had racked up a much more impressive forty-three. To my surprise, a few claimed they got all fifty questions right. I assumed some were jokers, but others were adamant.

GENUINE 50 OUT OF 50. NO JOKE.

No quizmaster likes to think they've created an easy quiz, but if they'd got them all right, I couldn't complain. One or two perfect scores out of almost two hundred thousand teams, minimum, wasn't anything to be ashamed about.

As I began wrapping up, I raised the sixty-four-thousand-dollar question.

I promised I'd sort out the technical glitches, in particular the scrolling comments section where people could see others writing answers. I'd also make the questions a tiny bit less UK-centric in recognition of the global audience that I seemed to have drawn. If I did that, would people be interested in me doing more quizzes, maybe even make it a regular Thursday night event?

The answer was instantaneous. And it was accompanied by comments that left me close to tears.

Please, please, please do it next week.

You're amazing, man! Really made our night! Keep it up!

Great quiz, thank you for taking the time to do this and keep the country and world going through these difficult times.

Paige had already shown me a few offers of help that had come in with moderating the comments and advising me on the tech side of things. It was obvious that it was a big enterprise and would need extra hands, so I said I'd take whatever was going.

I wrapped up the quiz with another flurry of thank yous. A part of me was almost reluctant to leave because I could see that some people were now playing the quiz 'as live' and would be able to do so whenever they wanted from tonight onwards. But I eventually logged out of YouTube and switched off the computer. I leaned back in my chair and punched the air. Sarah gave me a big hug, as did Paige.

The quiz had lasted for a little over an hour and a half, so it was around 9.30 p.m. by the time I wrapped it all up. I was still on a high, so Sarah, Paige and I sat together to cool down, do a post-mortem and generally let the adrenaline levels settle back to normal. It wasn't easy.

I flicked through my phone at the messages that had been pouring in through the night. They were all congratulatory, but there was also some light-hearted ribbing from my old quiz mates. They had always kept me grounded and I knew I'd need them to do that again now, so I was glad to see Haydn, Gareth, Roy, Ryan, Ste and Sal still taking the mickey out of me.

'No mention of Andi Peters?' one of them joshed, referring to my most infamous mistake from my early days as a pub quizmaster.

It was a couple of other emails that really put the events of the past few days and hours into perspective though.

One friend pointed out that YouTube had a special award, the Silver Play Button trophy, for having more than 100,000 subscribers to a channel. It was considered a real feather in the cap and YouTubers spent years working away to achieve this. I was already way over the threshold to achieve it – I had 140,000 subscribers and rising when I last looked. I'd done that in the space of a few days. And without really trying at all. I hadn't spent a penny on promotion or advertising. It had just happened. I'd heard the word 'viral' bandied around on the internet over the years and seen a few silly pranks and cat memes take off with zillions of views on YouTube and elsewhere. But I'd never really appreciated what it meant. I certainly hadn't considered how it happened, or what it must feel like. Now I knew. Well, partly. The *how* was still a complete mystery to me. But I knew that it felt mind-blowing. Surreal. Too much to take in properly.

The other message that stopped me in my tracks was from another friend.

He was a bit of a nerd and had been going through the listings to see what else had been on TV that night at 8 p.m. It had been serious fare, not surprising given all that was happening in the world. The BBC was showing the magazine programme *The One Show* and then a special edition of the current affairs forum *Question Time*. Neither had an audience or guests of any kind, of course. Everyone participated via Zoom. ITV was showing news and the popular soap *Emmerdale*, while BBC Two had *Saving Lives at Sea*, a documentary about the brave men and women who piloted the coast's lifeboats. Elsewhere, the only really light-hearted alternative was *The Dog Rescuers* on Channel 5. Channel 4 and BBC Four both had news. The only quiz alternative was a rerun of an old episode of the massively popular *The Chase* with Bradley Walsh on ITV4. My friend had done some sums based on the audiences those channels normally pulled in and compared it with the figure we might

have had based on the half a million or so teams that had participated that night.

'I reckon you were one of the top ten most viewed things on
during that hour and a half,' he wrote. 'Easily in the top ten, maybe
higher. Top five.'

I shook my head quietly. Everything else was the stuff of fantasy,
but this was utterly ridiculous. How on earth had that happened?

Sarah and Paige went to bed around midnight, leaving me to
continue winding down on my own. I was grateful for a little time
alone with my thoughts. I felt pretty mellow, mainly thanks to the
gin. The effects had begun to hit me now. I'd regret it first thing in
the morning when Jack woke me up.

I put my phone to one side and went and sat in the garden, something I liked to do when I wanted to chill out. It was a clear, moonlit
night and the stars were out, although there was a stiff breeze
building.

The streets of Darwen were as quiet as the grave. I sat back in
one of our garden chairs and tried to decompress and take stock. I
felt a curious mix of exhaustion, excitement, pride, relief and disbelief swirling around inside me. I kept smiling to myself, shaking my
head in wonder at it.

But, me being me, there was soon a flood of questions too.
There was the format of the quiz. My performance. Why hadn't
I anticipated people putting answers in the comments section?
Had the mix of questions been OK? I certainly couldn't make
them quite so UK-centric next time. And what had people really
thought of me? Was my presentation style OK? Then there was
the question of what lay ahead. What would the reaction be to
what had happened? Would the press pick up on it tomorrow?
Or would I quietly fade from the headlines? And when would I
do the next quiz? Next Thursday? Or should I do a second one
sooner? In case another quizmaster suddenly appeared and
stole my thunder? In case my audience melted away as quickly
as it came?

As my mind continued to run away with itself, I looked up at the stars, partially obscured now by a bank of cloud being blown towards the Pennines by the breeze. Staring at the night sky often made me think of my grandad. I often sensed his presence. He'd got me through some tough times. The toughest, in fact. I hoped he'd been looking down tonight. I hoped he was proud of me.

I knew what he would be saying if he heard me asking all these what-ifs. If I tried hard enough, I could probably hear him saying it. 'Jay, you achieved something amazing. Enjoy the moment. Tomorrow is another day. *Que sera, sera.*'

As the breeze stiffened and the thickening clouds turned the night a few shades darker, I headed indoors, smiling to myself.

He was right, of course.

8

BACKSTREET BOY

True or false, all bats are nocturnal?
Jay's Virtual Pub Quiz No 22, May 2020

What colour is the District Line on the London Underground map?
Jay's Virtual Pub Quiz No 3, April 2020

Complete the name of the newspaper/movie
character: *The Secret Life of ___ Mitty?*
Jay's Virtual Pub Quiz, One Year Anniversary Quiz, March 2021

On my first morning on the Embankment I woke up early, around six. The view from my bench could have been the opening shot in a movie. The first hint of the sunrise was visible to the east and the skyline, from St Paul's to the glass towers of the City of London beyond it, was layered with pinks, greys and pale blues. The river was eerily calm; not a vessel was moving along the water.

Shaking off the last remnants of sleep, I felt at peace too. I'd slept surprisingly well for five or six hours, undisturbed. And I'd woken feeling as if a weight had been lifted off my shoulders. As if I'd found some kind of equilibrium. For now, at least.

I was still lying on the bench when I saw a couple of early-morning joggers moving towards me along the riverbank, a hundred yards or so away.

In my head, I'd persuaded myself I wasn't another homeless person. I was simply sleeping out in the open. Here at my new home, at No 3 Riverside View. So I quickly slipped out of my sleeping bag and began stuffing my belongings into my little rucksack, ready to head off.

Of course, it was obvious that I'd slept there. The sleeping bag was a bit of a giveaway. But to me, it was important that I tried to present a different picture. Silly as it sounded, I wanted the runners to believe that I too was at the start of my day. I had a purpose, somewhere to go. People to see, business to get on with.

One of the joggers was too wrapped up in the music blaring through his headphones to acknowledge me, but when I nodded at them the other made a small gesture with his hand. As they drew away, I followed them, walking in the same direction, west towards Embankment Tube station and Hungerford railway bridge. Towards central London. To get on with the business of my day.

*

Since that light-bulb moment on the bus the previous day, my mission had become clear. I was going to live day by day, starting and ending it here at the bench and taking what happened in between as it came. I didn't think of it as survival. I thought of it more as a challenge. A daily test of my wits, resilience and resourcefulness. But it was also an opportunity to have some freedom. To live without rules or expectations of any kind. From anyone.

I can see now how I must have been thinking at the time.

My life had been so unstable, so troubled by assorted issues, from the bust-up with my mum, to Christina, to the periods of unemployment. I'd needed to simplify things. I'd needed a life with minimal involvement with others. A life I could lead on my own terms. I hadn't thought through the repercussions. How it might affect me. Except to think, as I'd done the night before, that whatever was going to happen to me was going to happen. I'd accept it. *Que sera, sera.*

*

Of course, it wasn't going to be easy. I no longer had any form of income. Technically, I suppose, I was eligible for unemployment benefit. Given my mental state, I would probably be able to claim something more. But I figured it would be too complicated. There would be too much red tape, too many questions. And rules.

So my job now was to walk the streets, scavenging for the things I needed to make it through each day. Any bits of loose change. Any uneaten or discarded takeaway meals. Clothes too. I'd brought only a couple of T-shirts, a jumper and a few pairs of socks with me. I only had one pair of trousers. Being able to travel on the Underground and on buses was also going to be crucial, especially when the weather turned colder. So my other main task was to look out for discarded travel passes and tickets. I soon turned that into a fine art.

I'd head for popular tourist Tube stations like Covent Garden, Oxford Circus and Leicester Square or the main railway stations like Waterloo, Charing Cross, King's Cross and Victoria. Tickets were often dropped or abandoned near the automatic barriers or booth windows. Occasionally I'd find one stuck in a machine, where someone must have – for whatever reason – walked away without the ticket.

In some ways, I was like one of those treasure hunters with their metal detectors. Mining for gold. An Oyster card could be a worthwhile find. It was always a throw of the dice when I tapped the card on the Oyster machine. If I was lucky, it would be charged up to twenty pounds, but more often than not the cards had been discarded with pennies left on them, which made them next to useless. Rail tickets with a specific destination were better, although they didn't give you the freedom to go where you wanted. The ultimate prize was a Travelcard that allowed you to travel to all six zones of the London Underground and bus networks. From Heathrow in the west to Romford and beyond into Essex in the east. I called it the Holy Grail.

I began to work out the best ways of spinning out a Travelcard so that it lasted an entire day. The longest journey you could take by bus was from Paddington to Romford. It was an hour and a half. I'd then get back on another bus at Romford and head into town – if I was really lucky, with a takeaway meal that someone had left on the bench at the station when their bus turned up. During those first weeks, that happened a couple of times and the hour-long journey back into town with a warm meal had been a real treat. I'd curled up at No 3 content as a baby.

Planning helped, but I learned that persistence too was key. Often, I walked up to fourteen hours a day. I'd walk loops around the city, sometimes starting off to the east, perhaps heading to Tower Bridge and then north to Islington and across to Paddington via the Regent's Canal. Or west, out through Victoria down the King's Road through Chelsea and then out to Putney and on to Hammersmith. If I'd found a Holy Grail, I'd travel out to Heathrow and walk around there. I was a bit of a plane spotter, so would sit and watch the air traffic taking off and landing for a few hours. I rarely got bored. Quite the opposite. If you're tired of London, you're tired of life, the old saying goes. It is an endlessly fascinating place. You never know what's around the next corner. Or who you'll see on your travels.

During those first months, I became a semi-professional people watcher. I'd entertain myself by working out the stories of those who shared the train or bus carriages with me. I would never engage or approach people, of course. So, as far as I was concerned anyway, the pictures I painted in my head were always right because I'd never find out what the actual answers were. I'd see a smartly dressed, middle-aged lady with a posh Prada handbag and I'd imagine her going home to her husband and children to a nice house in the Middlesex suburbs. I'd see her cooking a fancy dinner and having a glass of wine.

I'd see people on the Piccadilly line heading out to Heathrow with suitcases. I'd imagine them going off on holidays and business trips. To Florida or Fuerteventura. To Rome or Rio de Janeiro. Sometimes I'd see a young guy in a suit looking edgy and nervous.

I'd imagine him in a job like I'd had years earlier at Carphone Warehouse. I'd picture him leaving the train and walking into his manager's office and having to explain why his sales figures for that month were below par. I had a pretty good idea how he felt. In cases like that, I'd bizarrely feel sorry for people. Not just because of the pressure I knew they must be under or the fact they were like rats on a wheel, endlessly trying to get somewhere they were never going to get. But I also felt sorry for them because they didn't know how fragile their existence really was. What was the old saying? Everyone was only a couple of pay cheques away from homelessness. The scary thing was – it was the truth. Anyone could fall through the cracks. Anyone could end up like me.

Occasionally, I'd see someone who made me dwell on my own fortunes, how I'd ended up here. It might be some dapper executive in a smart suit getting on the Central line at Bank. Or a super-fit-looking young guy or girl getting on in their tracksuit on the way to the gym. It might be the way a particular person spoke or the expensive shopping bags they were carrying. It might be the way someone exuded confidence or calm or just sheer coolness. I'd wonder whether there was a way that my life might have ended up like theirs. Whether, if I'd had some good fortune or made a different turn, I could have ended up in their shoes. What if I'd stayed at McDonald's? I might be a senior management executive by now. What if I'd stayed with Christina in the north-east? I might have started my own business. The fact of the matter, of course, was that I had made the decisions I had. I'd been dealt the hand I'd been dealt. I had no choice but to play it.

★

I had a few guiding principles during this period. Firstly, I didn't want to stand out. I wanted to blend into the crowds when I was walking down Oxford Street or Tottenham Court Road. So I tried to keep myself tidy. I didn't want to look like some of the roughest characters I saw on the streets. If I found 20p, I'd sometimes use it to get access to a decent toilet at the main railway stations, where I'd try and have a wash. I'd begun to grow a light beard years earlier, but did my best to keep it tidy by picking up cheap razors when I could.

I tried to look presentable too, so I was always on the lookout for cast-off clothes, and did surprisingly well early on. I found a decent waterproof jacket discarded outside a charity shop near London Bridge. I soon learned to look out for skips or large industrial bins that had been left uncovered. You never knew what you'd come across.

I found a lot of my entertainment this way too. I'd find copies of daily newspapers and spend time doing crossword or number puzzles each day. Sometimes I'd find a discarded book or magazine. Occasionally I'd buy a cheap book in a charity shop. I was a Harry Potter fan and had read and listened to audio versions of all the books in the series before taking to the streets. Not long after I'd arrived on the streets, in July, I bought a copy of *Harry Potter and the Deathly Hallows*. I lay on the bench, hearing Stephen Fry, Daniel Radcliffe and the familiar voices from the audio books and the films in my head as I read. It helped pass many a long hour that first summer.

It was towards the end of that summer that I found a little radio with headphones. It was an old model, and its batteries were dead. But when I'd scraped together enough money, I fitted new batteries and got it working. It was a godsend. It transformed my life and – to my mind, anyway – provided me with a link to the outside world. I was careful to ration my use. Batteries were expensive. But I'd listen to the radio on the bench in the evening, tuning in to BBC news programmes sometimes but also entertainment shows like the *Round Britain Quiz* and *I'm Sorry I Haven't a Clue*. By day, I spent most of my time in the company of my favourite DJ, Chris Moyles.

At that time, he was the most popular DJ in the country. Millions listened to his daily show on Radio 1, but I felt like he was talking directly to me. I'd often respond to him as if we were having a conversation. It was just me and Chris, as far as I was concerned. We were sort of friends.

I'd made the decision to live off-grid, to live by my own rules. Day by day. From hand to mouth. Opportunity by opportunity. And during those early months, it felt good when I achieved it. Finding a five-pound note or a Holy Grail Travelcard produced an adrenaline rush. I learned to reward myself with treats. A bottle or tin of fizzy drink. Or, best of all, a packet of my favourite biscuits, custard creams. I could have lived on them, and occasionally did.

But what I didn't realise, of course, was that I was paying a price for this strange existence. From this withdrawal from society. While I walked the streets during the day, I didn't make eye contact. I didn't speak to anyone. I moved around in a kind of trance. I just kept my head down. Lost in my own thoughts. Looking for money, tickets or food. As a result, the parts of my personality that I used for normal social interaction were being switched off. I was gradually losing my ability to function as a member of society. I was also losing my identity, my self. Instead, I began living in my still over-active imagination.

It's strange how the human psyche works. It is a form of survival, I can see now, looking back at that time. You create your own reality. I guess it had to be that way. The true reality was too relentlessly grim. So, rather than fraternising with my fellow humans, I began to live a vivid fantasy life.

It was a few weeks into my stay at No 3 that I first sensed my grandad's presence. I wasn't particularly a believer in ghosts or spirits or the supernatural in any way. And, looking back on it now, I can see that it may well have simply been a side-effect of my mental unravelling. Some kind of self-protective projection my brain was making as I struggled to adjust to a world without human contact. But, regardless, I saw him sitting at the other end of the bench, peacefully looking out at the river. He turned and smiled at me, as he used to when I was a boy. 'All right, Jay.' From then on, I spoke to him frequently.

I would tell him what my plans were. 'I'm going to walk to Hammersmith today, Grandad.' Or I would ask him for advice. 'There's rain coming and I need a coat. Where would be the best place to find some cast-offs, Grandad?' Sometimes he'd answer. I'd hear a voice. Other times, I'd just sense his physical presence. A few times, standing at the junction of a street in central London torn about which direction to take, I felt a gentle pressure on me, pushing me one way or the other. I always told myself it was him. He'd been my guardian in life; he was still that in death.

I also began to have regular, more flamboyant flights of fantasy. It was Walter Mitty stuff. I'd see a flashy sports car – a Ferrari or a Lamborghini, maybe – and I'd immediately be Lewis Hamilton or Michael Schumacher. I'd imagine myself at the wheel, steering the car around the streets of Monaco or through the night during the Le Mans 24 Hour Race. I'd hear the voice of Murray Walker, the TV racing commentator. 'And there goes Jay Flynn, flying through the chicane.'

I'd walk past a pub or a TV showroom while a football match was on and I'd picture myself playing for Spurs alongside the stars of the current side, Dimitar Berbatov, Robbie Keane and Jermaine Jenas. I'd see myself making a mazy run and sliding in a goal at home at White Hart Lane and the fans chanting my name.

My fantasies often had an element of theatre to them. One day, walking through Covent Garden, for instance, 'Everybody' by Backstreet Boys was playing in my headphones. The piazza was packed with tourists and street performers. I began singing to myself. Suddenly, I imagined a scene from a musical, the entire crowd following my lead and singing along with me, trailing behind me as if I was some Pied Piper. A real, if rather dishevelled Backstreet Boy. God only knows what those who saw me thought of this strange character singing and smiling to himself. I guess they'd have simply added me to the cast of eccentrics and oddballs who populate central London. I probably didn't stand out that much at all.

I can see now that I was feeding a need deep within me. I guess it's in us all. Some inner child. Filling a gap that, at some level, we all have. Mine was a vast, gaping void.

Inevitably, the life I was leading took its toll on my mental state. There were times when I felt almost high on the simplicity of my life. When I felt euphoric at finding a Holy Grail. Or a half-eaten burger outside McDonald's or Burger King. I had nights when I felt completely at ease, lying on the bench at No 3 listening to the radio, in touch with the world yet disconnected from it at the same time. In my happy place. Amazingly, during my first months, I wasn't bothered or harassed by anyone while I slept overlooking the Thames.

But there were times when the reality of my situation came crashing back in. When I realised how empty my life had become. It was then that the suicidal thoughts returned.

Late in that first summer, I saw an advert for the Eastbourne Air Show. It stirred up happy memories of when my grandad had taken me to an air show in Southend as a kid. We'd stayed at the apartment of a friend of his from the film business. I'd loved every second of it. I could still picture an old Spitfire sputtering its way across the blue skies, to cheers from the vast crowds on the beach below.

I decided to head to the south coast for the weekend. To see the show.

I had an ulterior motive.

I'd had a bad run at 'work'. I'd failed to find any worthwhile tickets and very little money. I'd gone a couple of days here and there where I'd barely eaten. All I'd been able to do was sleep, but even that had been difficult. I'd been moved on from Hyde Park and even No 3 Riverside View had become a problem. A road sweeper from Westminster City Council had twice given me a dig in the ribs early in the morning.

'Move on, mate. You can't sleep there,' he'd said.

On another occasion, I'd somehow overslept – badly. I'd woken up on a bright day, aware of something landing on my sleeping bag.

I cleared the sleep from my eyes and took a look. They were small pebbles. A couple more arrived. I looked around and saw a large group of schoolchildren gathered a short distance up the Embankment, waiting for a coach. They were laughing guiltily and pointing at me. To my horror, I saw on Big Ben that it was one o'clock in the afternoon. I'd slept all through the morning. It had unsettled me and made me wonder whether my ideal home was quite so ideal after all. So as I set off on foot for Eastbourne, a familiar train of thought had already taken hold in my mind. I'd see how I felt when I got there. I might revive my idea of half a dozen years earlier and go to Beachy Head.

It took me four days to walk the sixty or so miles to Eastbourne. I set off through south-east London past Brands Hatch racetrack in Kent. I then veered down through Kent, moving past Tunbridge Wells and through the green expanse of countryside that led to the coast.

To my surprise, it was easier to find places to sleep in the countryside. On two nights I slept in old wooden bus stops in small villages. Buses were few and far between, so I had the little wooden constructions to myself. They were pretty comfortable and well sheltered. On the other night, I slept in some bushes within woodland. I was disturbed a couple of times by the sound of animals nearby. I wasn't sure what they were, but I wasn't worried.

I reached Eastbourne the day before the air show. Every spare inch of land around the town was already filling up with tents, caravans and camper vans. There was a real party atmosphere, not that I was invited or would have accepted the invitation if it had come. I had only managed a couple of washes in service stations on the way down from London so wasn't in my most hygienic state. I found a very comfortable enclosed bench at the far end of the seafront and spent the night there.

The air show was spectacular. The Red Arrows formation team did a fly-past; an array of old Second World War bombers and fighter planes criss-crossed the skies. I whooped and cheered along with the crowds. It was a real adrenaline rush. It took me back to my childhood. It may well have saved my life.

When you are in that kind of state mentally, your moods oscillate wildly from despair to elation, calm to anxiety, often in the space of moments. I've never been diagnosed with bipolar but it is, I guess, a form of that. Combined with the impulsive side of my nature, it can make for a dangerous cocktail. I have often frightened myself by the impulses that have flashed through my mind. This time, it worked positively.

I had such a great time watching the air show that all thoughts of walking to Beachy Head vanished. Instead, I was filled with a weird optimism. I realised life wasn't so bad after all. It was worth living. I heard my grandad again. He was telling me that I shouldn't give up hope.

Almost on autopilot, I packed up my few belongings, slung my rucksack on my shoulder and began the long walk back from Eastbourne to London.

★

It was all so impulsive, and just underlined how volatile I still was. I was prone to all sorts of ideas. Walking a knife-edge at times. One Sunday in October that year, for instance, I was scanning the concourse at Paddington station, on the lookout, as usual, for coins or a discarded travel pass. I was quite excited when I found an unused rail ticket. To my mild amazement, it was an open return to Penzance in Cornwall. Three hundred miles away.

It threw me for a moment.

What should I do?

It was an expensive ticket but there was no name on it. The main ticket office was closed and the skeleton Sunday staff members all looked busy.

I found a timetable mounted on a wall. A train was leaving in twenty minutes' time. It was a five-hour trip and would arrive in Penzance late in the afternoon.

I weighed it up for a moment. The weather wasn't great in London and there were storms predicted that afternoon and evening.

At least I'd be dry for five hours. And do I have anything better to do? The answer was obvious.

I boarded the rather impressive express train and found myself a comfortable seat in a quiet carriage. The train was soon easing its way out of the station and through west London.

I settled down. It was a treat to be on such a luxurious train and the gentle rattling and swaying as we sped along soon sent me to sleep. I've discovered since that the journey from London to Cornwall is one of the prettiest train trips in the UK. It passed me by. I woke up as we were pulling into Penzance late on that Sunday afternoon.

It reminded me of Rochester in many ways. It's a historic, slightly run-down town with a network of narrow cobbled streets near the water – in this case, the open sea. In the summer the place would have been alive with tourists, but at this time of the year it was deadly quiet. Some of the pubs and restaurants were closed, only a few people were out and about. None of them paid me much attention.

I found a small convenience store open and bought myself some biscuits. I took a walk to the seafront and sat watching the sea for a while. It was a beautiful part of the world, of that there was no doubt.

There were no more trains back up to London so I was going to have to stay the night here. I began sussing out the town and found an alleyway where, I figured, I could probably spend the night. I only had a couple of pounds on me.

As I strolled around the town, my mind began to tick into action. The train ticket was valid for a month. *This is a nice place. What if I stay here for three or four weeks? To see if it might be a viable option?*

The pros were soon being outweighed by the cons. It was October now, there wouldn't be much life here for another six months, maybe more. Even if there was work, I had no ID or anything to prove who I was or what experience I'd had. That was a non-starter, I figured.

Living the same hand-to-mouth existence I did in London wasn't an option either. In London, I could walk the streets for sixteen hours a day without going down the same road, in search of money or food or Travelcards. Where was I going to find anything here?

I settled down in the alleyway and slept most of the night, sitting upright. The first train left a little after seven o'clock. I bought a small packet of biscuits to get me through the journey back to London and headed for the station.

As Penzance disappeared into the distance, I was already looking forward to being back in London. I missed my home town. I missed my home. I felt safer there. More sure of myself, in a way. It made no sense, but it was the truth. My truth, at least.

My first Christmas was a weird experience. The weather had turned much colder by now and I had to spend more time indoors, usually on the Tube, where I could stay warm for most of the day. But I also walked the streets a lot and had a front-row seat as central London was transformed into a festive wonderland. One day I watched a team of riggers erecting the elaborate lights over Oxford Street and Regent Street. In Trafalgar Square, I looked on as the traditional Norwegian tree was being hauled into position. As December got underway, the pubs and bars began to buzz with parties. Oxford Street and the West End was busy with shoppers and tourists taking in the seasonal shows. It was an early Christmas present for me, in a way. There was more money on the streets. Literally.

A week or so before Christmas, the weather had turned arctic, so I'd decided to walk through the night to stay warm. I'd aim to sleep during the day, when the Tubes and buses were running. I'd headed towards Marble Arch and then walked down Park Lane. It was unusually quiet. I was walking along the western side of the road, on the opposite side to the grand hotels, The Dorchester, Grosvenor

House and the Inn on the Park, when I saw something fluttering in the breeze. It took me a moment to realise it was a bank note of some kind. I stepped out into the empty road to grab it. No sooner had I done so than I saw more notes. By now, I could see the headlights of several cars approaching. I did a weird kind of dance as I quickly grabbed one note then trapped another by stamping on it. I almost threw myself off the road as the cars drew close.

I was breathing heavily – it had been a little scary. But I saw that I had four ten-pound notes. Where had they come from? Had some high-rolling gambler thrown them in the air coming out of a casino in nearby Mayfair? Had the notes just flown out of the wallet of some drunken partygoer leaving one of the hotels? Or was it my grandad's doing? Had he steered me there, knowing this little windfall was waiting? I had no idea. Nor did I care much.

On the way back to the Embankment, I popped into an all-night convenience store and treated myself to a sandwich, a fizzy drink and some custard creams. The next day, I used virtually all the money to buy myself a woolly jumper and a couple of thermal-style vests in a charity shop. I had a decent wash and shave at Charing Cross railway station toilets too. It made me feel better, less self-conscious of my appearance. My Christmas had definitely come early.

My first Christmas Day on the streets caught me off-guard. I hadn't really counted on the fact that everything would be closed. Bizarrely, the only place I found open was a Starbucks on Oxford Street. I had no more than a pound on me, so I managed to persuade one of the staff to give me a cup of hot water then helped myself to a teabag that was still sitting in a cup on a table on the way out.

The weather was unseasonably warm and Hyde Park was busy in the afternoon, filled with people walking off the excesses of their Christmas lunches, I assumed. I watched them walking by as I finished mine, a packet of custard creams I'd been stretching out for several days now.

As I sat there on a bench nibbling away, I didn't have any real regrets. I didn't feel sorry for myself. I wasn't jealous in any way of the families or the couples walking romantically arm in arm. I'd made the choices I'd made. Christmas was a time for friends and family. As far as I was concerned, I didn't really have those. I barely gave my mother, sister and brother a second thought. I was content to be on my own.

My main aim was to gather enough food and warmth to get through to Boxing Day, when the world reopened. Walking through Leicester Square I found a couple of coins, which would give me a good start the next day. I spent Christmas night on the bench, listening to the radio.

New Year's Eve was a more unsettling time, mainly because I had to share my bench with several thousand people.

I'd been travelling around all day and hadn't really given any consideration to the fact that it was New Year's Eve or that London was, as usual, staging a giant fireworks display on the Thames. People were pouring out of Embankment Tube station and making their way to the riverside. *My back garden is filled with thousands of people, none of whom I know,* I thought to myself.

For a while, I thought about staying put. But then I decided to go to Trafalgar Square and watch the display there instead. It was too crowded on the Embankment.

As the pyrotechnics went off at midnight and the skies lit up, I stared up blankly. If anyone had looked at me, they'd have seen the fireworks reflecting in a pair of eyes that were effectively dead to the world.

I walked around all night, past clubs and bars, homes and even gardens where people were celebrating the arrival of the New Year. One or two people shouted 'Happy New Year' at me. I didn't respond. Whether it was 2007 or 2008 didn't really make much difference to me. My world didn't have any shape to it. It didn't abide by the same boundaries as everyone else's. I was – in the main – content to be living apart. Cut off from the rest of humanity, even though I was surrounded by it.

If there was one moment that summed up my strange, disconnected state, it came early that second year, 2008.

I'd been walking around Oxford Street one morning, listening to Chris Moyles on the radio as I scoured the streets. He had been bantering with his colleagues about McDonald's, and complaining specifically about the fact that you couldn't get a breakfast after 11 a.m. 'Why do McDonald's stop doing breakfast at 11 a.m.?' It annoyed him – and a lot of his listeners – that if you turned up at 11.05 a.m., you couldn't get a breakfast McMuffin.

'If anyone knows, get in touch,' he'd said.

'It's obvious,' I said to myself, as if talking to him.

It must have been fate, because I was near Margaret Street and within a couple of minutes of the BBC studio near Broadcasting House where Chris recorded his show.

Chris often referred in his show to the fact that he slipped out during his breaks to have a cigarette in the street. It was just coming up to the news on the half hour so I suspected he may be taking a break at that precise moment. I hadn't run anywhere for years, but I moved as fast as I could in that direction, weaving my way through the back streets and dodging the shoppers heading for Oxford Street.

My hunch had been correct. I arrived to find Chris Moyles standing on the pavement on the other side of the road, smoking a cigarette with a colleague.

I have no idea how I must have looked. But I didn't care. I shouted across the road.

'Chris. You can't have breakfast at McDonald's after 11 a.m. because the grills are switched to a different temperature to cook burgers. And some people are allergic to eggs as well, so you can't cross-contaminate.'

He and his colleague looked across, utterly baffled. Their faces were a picture. *Who is this person, shouting across the street?* I gave him a thumbs-up sign, then turned on my heel and headed back towards Oxford Street.

When Chris returned on air, he was laughing.

'The strangest thing just happened to me,' he said. 'I was outside having a smoke and some random bloke just shouted out the answer to that question about McDonald's. And then shot off.'

It became a running gag for the rest of the show.

To a normal, well-adjusted person, it would have seemed like very weird behaviour. A normal person would have called in or texted. Or if they had found themselves face to face with a famous radio presenter, they would have introduced themselves, asked for a selfie or an autograph. There was a time when I might have done that. But that wasn't the way I thought any more. It epitomised a contradiction at the heart of my life. I'd convinced myself that I didn't want to be part of society. That I wanted to remain cut off. Yet at a basic, human level, I actually craved interaction of some kind. I needed validation, recognition, whatever you want to call it. I needed to be seen. Even though I wanted to be invisible at the same time. It would take a while longer for me to square that circle, to work my way through this. At the time, however, I was oblivious to it all. Instead, I was on a high afterwards and still buzzing when I settled down on the bench that night. I kept laughing to myself. I'd been the source of a little bit of light entertainment for millions.

I sensed the familiar presence, sitting alongside me in the moonlight.

'It's not every day they talk about you on the BBC, is it, Grandad?' I said, still grinning from ear to ear.

9

QUIZZIE RASCAL

Who entertained the nation with PE lessons
during the 2020 UK lockdown?
Jay's Virtual Pub Quiz No 16, May 2020

Who is Bob the Builder's business partner?
Jay's Virtual Pub Quiz No 4, April 2020

The morning after the quiz, the headline story on the BBC's main news website read: *Coronavirus: Thousands join Jay Flynn's virtual pub quiz.*

According to the report, 340,000 people had taken part on YouTube and Facebook, but I knew for a fact that figure was already old news.

At breakfast time, I saw there were four hundred new people playing the quiz live at that precise moment alone. A couple of thousand more had played overnight. I shook my head, the reality and scale of what had happened hitting me afresh. Who was playing at this time of the day? And where? And when – if ever – would they stop?

As I'd feared, the gin I'd drunk the previous night had left me with a sore head. The hangover wasn't helping me deal with the contradictory thoughts flying around once again. On the one hand, I was genuinely thrilled that the quiz was being seen as a success. The flip side was that I was now in the public domain. The BBC report was only one of many online. My phone was alive with texts and emails from friends who had heard my name that morning on radio and TV news bulletins.

'You won't be able to walk around the supermarket,' Sarah had joked over breakfast. 'Good thing you'll be hidden behind a face mask,' Paige had added.

I could only smile half-heartedly. I didn't find it funny. Sooner or later, someone was going to use the f-word and say I was now famous. That didn't sit comfortably with me.

The weight that I'd felt lifting briefly at the end of last night had returned. It was a burden of expectation. But also a fear of the unknown. My email inbox only underlined the feeling. It was filled with thousands of messages. Who were they from? How on earth was I going to get through them?

I knew myself well enough to know I could easily be overwhelmed. So when Paige offered to weed her way through all the emails and begin doing some work on designing a logo, I agreed to take a break for a couple of hours. Forget the f-word, I was going to have to cope with the d-word too. Delegation. And accept the help I'd always found so difficult.

Jack had been asleep throughout the previous night's excitement. As far as he was concerned, I was the same person who had put him to bed and then greeted him when he'd woken up that morning. So I put my phone away and took the opportunity to spend some time with him.

It was a bright spring day so we played outside in our little garden. Watching Jack climb up and down his slide, chatting and smiling without a care in the world, was just the tonic I needed. Everything had changed, but nothing had changed. I was still a dad and a husband, and I had to get on with doing those jobs. Being 'present' in Jack's life was more important to me than anything. What was the old biblical saying about the sins of the father being visited on their sons? I told myself I wasn't going to allow that to happen. No matter where this crazy new venture took me.

By the late morning, I felt recharged and ready to face up to the monster I'd created. My immediate priority was to start preparing for the next quiz. I'd committed to it. I had to deliver.

It was going to look more professional, that was for certain. I knew Paige had a flair for art but hadn't realised she'd actually studied graphic design. She showed me some visual art she'd been working on. It was great, a striking logo in red and yellow for Jay's Virtual Pub Quiz. A friend of mine, Des, knew how to convert it into an online asset. I put them together to work on something that could be added to the Facebook and YouTube pages. It might take some time, but we'd be able to roll it out over the coming weeks.

Paige had also done a trawl through most of the emails, and she pointed out the ones she felt were a priority. They ranged from media organisations asking for interviews, to approaches from charities and companies offering to sponsor or get involved with me, to other quiz organisers asking for promotion.

Again, I felt conflicting emotions. It was brilliant that I had this much interest. I'd never known so much attention. But I was also intimidated by the prospect of teaming up with corporate and charity partners. I had no experience in their world. My imposter syndrome kicked in. I was just an idiot who had stumbled into a few hundred thousand people's living rooms. No major company was going to take me seriously, were they?

Among the messages was a note from a guy called Alex Holmes. He worked with The Diana Award, a charity inspired by the late Princess Diana dedicated to transforming the lives of young people, especially those who suffered bullying. His CV was very impressive.

We fixed up a call on Zoom.

He was a charming and smart guy. He was also really switched on and seemed to have a huge network of contacts. It was obvious that he was knowledgeable in lots of areas where I knew nothing. More importantly, I could also tell that he'd be trustworthy. And that I could work with him. Instinctively, I'd known I needed a partner. My gut told me I'd found one.

141

I liked a lot of what he had to say, in particular about using what he called my 'platform' to do good by raising money for charity. I'd benefited so much personally because of the existence of charitable organisations, sometimes small, under-appreciated operations that lived on a knife-edge financially. The idea of giving something back to such good causes really excited me. Alex also felt strongly that I should be earning some money from the quiz and mentioned a few options. Unlike the reality TV guy who'd called me before the first quiz, he wasn't suggesting I put everything behind a 'paywall'. Like me, he felt it would lose a huge chunk of my audience but also, crucially, just wasn't the right thing to do. 'People need things like this right now,' he said.

Instead, he showed me how I could start a patronage system, where quizzers could make a voluntary monthly contribution to help support me. It wouldn't stop anyone from playing the quiz for free. It would just allow people to show their gratitude by chipping in anything from a couple of pounds to maybe twenty quid a month to support me. I could take some of that and give it to charity myself, if I wanted to. There were lots of permutations.

I was still waiting to hear from Ian. I was growing less hopeful by the day that he'd be able to keep me on the payroll. Realistically, I knew I had to have a Plan B. But I was apprehensive.

British people – especially working-class ones – have a strange attitude to money. It's seen as very unBritish to talk about it, especially if it makes you seem greedy or money-grubbing. It doesn't bother other nationalities or those who have grown up with wealth, of course. It's odd. As someone who didn't come from money and had never really had any, I was nervous about being seen to be 'cashing in'. I told Alex I'd give it some thought. For now, I was much more excited about the charity fundraising. Generating money for other people was another matter entirely. I could handle that.

My overactive imagination kicked in and I began picturing a thriving organisation, some kind of community fund, helping different charities. I imagined us directly helping causes linked to children, homelessness, the environment and animals.

It wasn't that simple.

Over the next day or so I talked it through further with Alex, Sarah and Paige. Creating an official charitable fund would require a huge amount of administration, which wouldn't come cheaply. We'd have to hire premises, staff, register as a charitable organisation, be vetted and checked from top to toe. None of that particularly bothered me. What did I have to hide? But Alex raised the subject of vetting the charities who applied for funds. How would we do that? And what if we were the victims of some kind of scam, some fake charity? And what if we at the same time failed to give money to a charity that really deserved it?

We agreed instead to start work on a page on the JustGiving website, where all that work was effectively done for us. People could donate directly to our chosen charities, the NHS in particular. I was keen on fundraising for NHS Charities Together, a national charity co-ordinating support for the NHS workforce.

Alex said he was happy to help me promote this – and my quiz in general – on social media, especially Twitter, which, to be honest, was a bit of a mystery to me. He suggested I used the hashtag #VirtualPubQuiz. He reckoned he could get it 'trending' when I was live on Thursdays. Apparently, it was a way of building traffic. I took his word for it.

I was still really nervous about being seen to exploit the quiz's success in any way – even for charity – so that Saturday morning I put together a video on Facebook that explained my thinking. I wasn't pushing or pressing anyone to contribute. But I felt I couldn't ignore the potential to do some good that had been handed to me. To my relief, it got a universally positive response. People felt I should go for it. So – along with my newly assembled 'team' – we did.

★

The following few days flew by. In response to a few messages suggesting I do something for children, I put together a simple little quiz, which I pre-recorded and added to my YouTube channel on the Monday morning. I also started work on some specialist quizzes, which I'd begin to pre-record and add to the channel as and when I could. Fifty questions each on Disney and Harry Potter seemed a good place to start.

The children's quiz didn't attract the hundreds of thousands that the Thursday night quiz had, but I was pleased to see the number of views rising steadily through the week. One of my fears was that I'd be a one-hit wonder, that no one would return on Thursday night. It gave me hope that someone might.

As Paige and I continued our post-mortem on the previous week, I made some technical tweaks. To begin with, I decided to put the next one up exclusively on YouTube. Running it simultaneously on Facebook and YouTube was going to be rife with technical issues, especially if – as I hoped – it got a little bit more sophisticated. My internet at home wasn't stable enough to cope. Alex had a connection with YouTube in London and said they might be supportive. It might even provide us with some income, he explained.

I also learned how to disable the live chat on the screen. I didn't want a repeat of the previous Thursday, so I'd switch it off when I was asking the questions. As an extra precaution, I took up an offer from a friend of Paige's to moderate the comments during the course of the evening, to weed out anything unsavoury or libellous. I learned how to add slides with the questions and answers so that players could read them. Paige was at work designing them, along with some other 'cards' that I could insert at the beginning and during breaks. We'd use them to link to our designated charities, we agreed. By the time the next Thursday was looming into view, I felt like we'd made big strides. It was never going to be the world's most professional quiz – that was partly the point – but I hoped it wasn't going to feel quite so amateurish.

My concerns about my audience not returning were quickly forgotten. As I prepared to start the questions a little after eight o'clock on that second Thursday, I saw that again we already had more than a hundred thousand viewers. Once more, players were spread wide across the world. I noticed one guy who was in Tanzania but was playing against his family back in Wales.

The quiz passed off without any major catastrophes. Alex had joined us and had been pushing the hashtag #VirtualPubQuiz and had – apparently – got it trending, winning us lots more followers on Twitter.

The most controversial moment came when, during the half-time break, I sang happy birthday as a response to the scores of people who had asked for shout-outs. The reaction was generally positive.

What a lovely thing to do.

But there were a few negatives.

Tone deaf.

This is weaponised cringe.

Fortunately, the killjoys were in the minority.

Great quiz. Very professional this week. Well done, someone wrote on the comments section as I wrapped things up. I felt like I was getting the hang of this. We'd even had a positive response to the fundraising and generated more than £20,000. I was thrilled. I was doing good for others – and myself.

We both needed it.

★

As March merged into April, the COVID crisis deepened. It was frightening. The death rates announced in the daily government press conferences were chilling. By the second week of the month, more than nine hundred people were dying within each twenty-four-hour period in the UK. Even the Prime Minister was in intensive care with the virus. The news from around the world was bleaker still. The number of coronavirus cases worldwide had passed one million. Ten per cent of those cases – 100,000 people – had died. And the numbers were rising exponentially, forcing governments from Brazil to Italy, the US to Africa to extend their lockdowns. It was clear that, despite some murmurings about a relaxation of rules, we weren't going to be released from our captivity any time soon. Sarah is a pretty happy-go-lucky person but even she had begun to worry. She'd arrived at her office one day to find a sign saying: Do Not Enter. Awaiting Deep Clean. Someone within her clinic had tested positive and over the course of the next week, almost all her colleagues called in sick with COVID. She was convinced she'd catch it too, but hadn't shown any symptoms, thankfully.

Part of her job was talking to patients, especially those with cancer, just to check up on their medication and treatment. She'd spoken to one elderly man, a widower in his nineties, for an hour. The poor guy was all alone apart from his two Yorkshire terriers and a cleaner who was allowed to enter his house once a week and to whom he spoke through a door. It was the highlight of his week. It brought home to me the isolation and loneliness people were suffering. It also made me think that, perhaps, my quiz offered a similar outlet to some. Afterwards, I asked Paige to keep an eye out in future quizzes for comments from people who were on their own. We should try to reply and engage with them if we could.

There were a few slim signs of hope. The UK had apparently begun testing a potential vaccine, and tests to allow people to see whether they were carrying the virus were in the pipeline too. But with the mood growing grimmer, the need to cheer people up and distract them from the news was even greater. As a result, all sorts of heroes – some well-known, others not – had emerged in the past weeks.

A ninety-nine-year-old Second World War veteran, Captain Tom Moore, had raised millions for the NHS by walking a hundred laps around his home, dressed in his suit and military decorations. The fitness trainer Joe Wicks had become a household name, taking millions of people through daily workouts on YouTube every morning. Pop stars and musicians had been performing concerts in their kitchens, comedians were producing Zoom-based entertainment. In mid-April, Lady Gaga organised a global concert – One World: Together at Home – in which superstars from Taylor Swift and Paul McCartney to Elton John and The Rolling Stones performed in their gardens.

I'd never compare myself to them, but I felt like, in my own small way, I was doing my bit to keep people's spirits up. During the first three weeks of the month, as well as three more Thursday quizzes, I started adding live Saturday quizzes. They weren't as well attended, but that didn't bother me. I felt like I was helping people by offering a trivial alternative to the horrors unfolding in the world outside. A safe haven where the c-word was banned.

During that month, I heard a lot of well-known people talk about what they were doing and the impact this strange new environment was having on them. The one that struck me most was Martin Lewis, the well-known TV and radio money expert. He was working around the clock putting together guides and podcasts to help people in dire financial straits to survive the crisis. 'In some ways I feel like I've been preparing for this moment my whole life,' he said in an interview I heard, sounding quite emotional. As the month wore on, I began to feel more and more the same way.

★

By the end of April, I'd put out five live Thursday night quizzes and half a dozen specialist or children's quizzes on YouTube. I should have been relaxing, settling into the routine. But as I got ready for the sixth quiz on the night of 30 April, I was more nervous than I'd been even on the first night back in March. It wasn't altogether surprising, given how much was riding on tonight.

That morning, I'd received an email from Guinness World Records. We'd been in touch soon after the first quiz to see if we could register it as a record somehow. So many people had suggested it, I had to at least try. I hadn't really expected a response for a while. If there were records being broken at the moment, they were of a much grimmer nature.

The email explained that they'd accepted the category we'd suggested, the largest live-streamed pub quiz on YouTube. They had looked at the evidence I'd submitted and were satisfied. What they now needed was to see and verify live evidence of the size of my audience. In short, they had to put a number to it.

I had emailed back and forth with their team and they explained the logistics. They needed to have direct sight of the live viewing figures at the beginning, middle and end of the broadcast. For obvious reasons, they couldn't send a representative to sit in my room in Darwen, so instead they'd agreed that I could set up a camera that would sit behind me and show them my screen throughout the broadcast. That way, they could satisfy themselves I wasn't up to any jiggery-pokery.

I knew we'd break the record. Throughout April I'd continued to get audiences in six figures each Thursday. I wasn't being boastful, but there simply wasn't anything remotely as successful as my quiz out there. But I wanted it to be a respectable figure, as close as possible to the giant audience I'd had on the first Thursday night back in March.

So I put up a video on Facebook that morning, excitedly explaining why I needed my regular participants to tell as many of their friends and family as possible to join in that night. I was a bundle of nerves all day as I kept pinging friends to make sure they were tuning in. Every participant counted.

As if the knot of nerves in my stomach over the record attempt wasn't enough, something else was eating away at me as well.

After weeks of humming and hawing, of making long lists of pros and cons, I'd agreed with Alex to set up an official account on Patreon, a popular website that allows people – or patrons – to subscribe to and support online content creators by making monthly contributions. I'd resisted it for as long as I could, but now I didn't feel I had an option if I wanted to keep the quiz going.

Early in April, Ian had told me officially that I wasn't covered by the new furlough scheme the government had introduced to help companies survive. He was really apologetic, but I'd joined after the official cut-off date for employees. As soon as they reopened, he promised, he'd be back in touch, but for now his hands were tied.

The news had focused me. With the world still in lockdown, there weren't any other job opportunities out there. And even if there were, I'd created a situation where I didn't have a spare minute to look for a job in any case. Compiling my quizzes was hard work, especially when each one was being played – and scrutinised – by hundreds of thousands of people. I was working twelve or fourteen hours a day compiling, hosting and setting up the recordings. It had taken over my life, but I wasn't earning a penny. If I didn't have a wife and a child and a house to run, I'd have been more than happy to keep it that way. But I had all three. It just wasn't sustainable. So I had to see if I could turn my role as a quizmaster into a paid job.

It went deeper than that, of course. I'd found something I was good at and that I loved. I really wanted to do this full time.

Sarah and I talked about it long into the nights. She, as ever, backed me to the hilt. Chances like this didn't come up often in life, she said. I had to give it a go. I'd never forgive myself if I didn't.

With Alex's help, I looked at the Patreon site then kicked the concept around a little. I'd decided to give people five options. At the starter level, they could chip in £3 a month to become what I'd decided to call a Quizzie Rascal. (I'd heard a quiz team use it for their name once and rather liked it. I was a fan of Dizzy Rascal.) It gave patrons first access to any special events I might run and a vote on which charities benefited from my Patreon membership. As I wrote on the site, 'This will allow me to follow a path set in front of me that I had never in my wildest dreams thought could be possible and something positive to come out of this awful worldwide situation. If you can, this £3 will make the quiz my job!'

The next level was Quizzstory Maker at £5 per month. Anyone contributing this much would get access to an exclusive quiz each month. I also pledged that £1 from each would go into a charity fund. I added three more levels after that: Gold, Platinum and Super Quizzer. The latter cost £20 a month, half of which went to charity.

I'd added various incentives, from private quizzes to free copies of the quiz book that I was working on. Alex was already exploring the idea of approaching publishers. It seemed fair.

All in all, it seemed a fair exchange. Yes, I'd be paid, but I'd be raising money for charity – and giving people something they wanted. And needed, if many of the comments I had received were to be believed.

I sat down for the quiz that night with an extra-large glass of gin by my side. I announced the World Record attempt at the beginning. I knew that we had a record, regardless. But I wanted it to be a big figure. The counter was soon flying towards the 100,000 mark. As I got going with the first question – a very UK-centric one: 'Which TV show's theme tune asks if Mr Hitler is kidding?' – it was well over 150,000.

As I moved through the first three rounds, I felt happy. Even when I made a terrible blunder by asking 'Which golfer has won the most majors, Tiger Woods or Jack Nicholson?'

I THINK YOU MEAN JACK NICKLAUS YOU CLOWN, someone kindly corrected me.

The team at Guinness sent a couple of emails confirming all was going smoothly but I couldn't stop myself checking every now and again that the camera behind me was picking up the counter on my screen correctly. It was nerves. It was announcing the Patreon that was really worrying me.

Looking back on it, I can see why I was quietly terrified. My success stemmed from the fact that I was a down-to-earth, normal guy. The people's quizmaster, as someone jokingly referred to me. Would this look too slick? Too corporate? Would people think I was getting too big for my boots? Or that this had been my plan all along? I'd just pretended to be some guy who'd stumbled into this. I'd been 'on the make' all along.

Fortunately, I'd soon run out of time to dwell on it any more. As half-time drew near, I muttered to myself, *Que sera, sera, Grandad.*

My nervousness would have been obvious to everyone. I was hesitant and apologetic as I explained what I had decided to do and took them through the principle of my Patreon account. I had deliberately switched off the livestream comments. I couldn't have handled any negativity. I just needed to get this 'out there' and let the cards fall where they may. People would vote with their fingers. It would either fly or not. It was in their hands.

I emphasised again and again that the quiz would remain free to everyone. It was completely optional whether people wanted to support me or not. I wrapped up my little speech by sharing a link to the new Patreon page and left it on screen while I took the usual ten-minute break. I went straight outside to the garden to breathe in as much fresh air as I could. I was so anxious. I was terrified that I'd misjudged my audience, somehow overstepped the mark. As usual, my head was flooded with wild ideas and questions. Why would they pay me to write quizzes when all they need do is switch on Chris Tarrant or Bradley Walsh on their TV sets? Who had that kind of money to spare during an unprecedented economic crisis? Why couldn't I just settle for what I had?

What seemed like an eternity soon passed. I still had three minutes until I had to go back online. I sat back down at my desk and breathed hard. I had the Patreon page open on a tab on my browser. I hit refresh, expecting maybe half a dozen people to have signed up. I couldn't believe my eyes when the page loaded.

More than a thousand people had pledged money. And the number signing up was rising every time I hit refresh. By the time the break was up and I had to return to the screen, more than 1,500 people had pledged. It would be enough to buy new equipment, a new computer, I hoped. I wanted to put Alex and Paige on some kind of wage to recognise all the work they were putting in. All of that was possible. And I'd be able to pay myself a decent wage as well.

Until now, it had all seemed like just words. It wasn't real. But now, as I looked at the number of pledges rising and rising still, there was no doubt.

It caught me off-guard. As I stood next to my desk and looked at the newly refreshed Patreon site, the tears just came. I couldn't stop.

Sarah rushed in, concerned.

'What's wrong?' she said. I just pointed at the Patreon screen.

'Oh wow,' she said. 'That's great. You should be laughing, not crying, silly.'

She was right, of course.

My emotional state was quite obvious when I returned to the screen. I was still wiping away the tears. 'Technically speaking, a lot of you are now my employers,' I said, sniffling away.

After a minute or two of trying to hold it together as I thanked everyone, I told myself off.

Stop being emotional, Jay. Get on with the quiz.

It wasn't easy, especially given what was happening with the world record attempt at the same time. As I reached the end of the quiz, I checked the figure on my screen. I knew it had peaked at more than 180,000. An email from the Guinness people arrived, saying they'd recorded an audience of 182,513 but would confirm that with me officially in the next few days.

I'd not felt so emotionally wrung out since I'd started the quizzes a month earlier. There was so much to absorb. So much that had happened. It was the reaction to my Patreon page that had really knocked me for six. When I switched off that night, the number of pledges was nearing four thousand. I felt a fresh wave of emotion come over me.

Sarah knew me well enough to leave me to absorb the moment. She didn't need to tell me how proud she was of what I'd achieved. The look in her eyes told me that. So, once again, I went to sit out in the garden to calm down and take stock. It was spitting lightly with rain, but I didn't mind. It woke me up from my dream-like state, gave me a little more clarity. Made me appreciate the moment, and what it meant to me. Which was a lot.

All sorts of thoughts were racing through my head, many of them about what I could now do with the quiz. How I could expand it, make it even more professional. Do international editions. Create an app. A podcast. A TV show. The possibilities were endless. I would have to stop myself from getting too carried away, I knew that already.

As I watched the clouds drifting by, I managed to still my thoughts for a moment. Martin Lewis's words came back to me. It was as if my life too had been some kind of warm-up for this moment. As if all the false starts and failures had been laying a foundation. I'd often felt I'd been in the right place at the wrong time in my life. Or that fate hadn't been on my side at crucial moments, I'd had an unlucky bounce of the ball or been let down by others. I'd never quite found my place in the world but now, by a complete fluke, thanks to a freakish accident, here I was. Exactly where I wanted to be. Doing what I wanted to do. Being precisely what I wanted to be. A quizmaster.

I'd never felt anything like this before. I felt on top of the world.

ROUND FOUR

10

NEVER BE LONELY

Force is equal to what times acceleration?
Jay's Virtual Pub Quiz No 7, April 2020

In which city did Anne Frank write her famous diary?
Quiz 15, Jay's Virtual Pub Quiz Book 2

'Happy New Year. Well, as I'm still going, I decided to keep a diary as to my trials and tribulations.'

On 1 January 2009, as I began my third calendar year on the streets, I had a new distraction from the relentless, repetitive, hand-to-mouth routine.

I had bought a cheap, lined exercise book that day and began scribbling away on the top deck of a bus back from Hounslow in the west of London into the city. So began my rather chatty, excitable but also brutally honest stream of consciousness – littered with Bridget-Jones-style lists. That first diary entry that day, for instance, ended:

Money: £38ish, give or take.
Papers: Sun/Mail (both bought) so far.
Food: McD's breakfast/lunch, Sausages from Asda.

If you'd asked me at the time why I'd started writing it, I'm sure the answer would have been simple. It was a way to relieve the sheer boredom and emptiness of my day-to-day existence. It was something to do. But as I look back on it now, I can see that it signalled something deeper. More complex.

Crazy as it may seem, I think a part of me was proud of the resilience and resourcefulness I'd shown, of the surreal structure I'd managed to impose on my life in the eighteen months since I'd decided to live on the streets. A part of me wanted to chronicle that existence. For whom, I didn't know, but I wanted it to stand as some sort of record of what happened to me. Whether I survived or not. To outlive me, maybe.

But by January 2009, I'd reached the point too where I wanted – I needed – to share my experience with someone, anyone. Something was shifting within me. I'd chosen to speak to a diary – but, in truth, I wanted to restart my conversation with the world.

I only kept the diary going for three weeks or so. It was long enough to capture some insightful snapshots of the chaos, cruelty, black comedy and sheer vulnerability of my life. It also shone a light on my ever-changing state of mind. Perhaps most importantly, however, it coincided with the moment when that wider conversation began. When I decided to reconnect myself with society. To end my time as an outsider and step back inside.

*

My first entry was a story within itself. For a start, that £38 I had in my pocket was the most I'd had in a long, long time. It had come my way the previous night, New Year's Eve. I'd scribbled in the diary:

At around 10.30pm someone was smiling on me. I'd decided that the Embankment wasn't the place to watch the fireworks so I went for a wander and found myself on Oxford Street as usual but this time luck smiled on me and with no-one around two brilliant brand new £50 notes were in the gutter.

I'd celebrated my windfall in style that night with 'a Burger King' and 'an Upper Crust' sandwich. I'd done the same as the previous year and watched the fireworks in Trafalgar Square. Then, knowing No 3 wouldn't be a peaceful place to spend the night, I'd crashed out on the free Tube until 4 a.m.

The following day, New Year's Day, I splashed the cash.

My radio had stopped working back in December, which was a depressing blow. I relied on it. It was my one indirect link to the outside world. I'd tried fixing it, but to no avail. So, with my unexpected windfall, I excitedly headed to an Argos store on Tottenham Court Road to look for a replacement in their January sales. I found a nice one for £35. It had an MP3 player integrated into it, which meant when I wasn't listening to the radio, I could listen to downloaded music. With that in mind, I also spent £20 or so booking time at an internet café in Paddington. I was going to start downloading a library of songs to my new player. Last but not least, I'd bought my notebook and some pens at an Asda supermarket out towards Hounslow.

★

Reading my daily musings now, I am struck not just by the repetitive nature of my life but also the physical and mental rollercoaster that, by then, I'd been riding for eighteen months. On the 3rd of the month, for instance, I noted:

> *I'm not well, feel really run down … Literally made a mess of myself, which wasn't nice, but I blame Mcd[onald']s Marble Arch for not having their toilets open at 5am.*

Later that day, however, my spirits had been lifted by a session of downloading music at the internet café:

> *In an hour and a half managed to get over 100 songs on. Yay! Will go again tomorrow now I know which computer to use. Got 16hrs left to use before Friday.*

My song choices ranged from quite sentimental ballads to rap and some show tunes. Looking back at the list now, I wonder whether there was a subliminal message hidden within it. My songs included 'Boulevard of Broken Dreams' by Green Day, 'Can't Lose What You Never Had' by Westlife, 'Cash in My Pocket' by Wiley with Daniel Merriweather and 'Go Your Own Way' by Fleetwood Mac.

The weather was turning cold and I'd probably have begun to regret not spending some of my windfall on warm clothing if Lady Luck hadn't been smiling on me once more. I recorded later that day:

Found a new jumper today, gonna bloody need it, freezing at the moment.

I'd ended the day with the usual list:

Food: Chips (bought), custards (first for ages)
Money: 30p (found 5p in Romford)
Papers: Sun (found)
Travelcard: 1-2, Green Park (Piccadilly road), 9pm

The weather had soon turned really wintry, but that, bizarrely, had been a cause for a bittersweet kind of joy. The next day, 4 January, I wrote:

I need to find a way of putting some excitement into my life. I know this because I got giddy over the fact it's snowing. Not really settled in town, but out in Romford I'm sliding on the snow at 3 in the morning. Sad, sad, sad!

At least I was able to stay warm later in the day when I reported another stroke of sartorial luck:

Got a new jacket, which I'm wearing alongside all my other clothes cos I'm that bloody cold. New pair of trousers as well, not tried them yet. Spent majority of day wandering then found a holy grail travel card (1-6 zones) at lunch time, so went to sleep all day again. Internet tomorrow, if weather like this I'm gonna be there all day!

Food: Rich tea biscuits
Money: Nil
Travelcard: 1-6 (Eros)

It turned out the trousers were a 32-inch waist and were so loose on my now emaciated body that I needed a belt.

One of the other tracks I'd downloaded was 'Never Be Lonely' by The Feeling. There was definitely something ironic about that. When I'd begun my time on the street, I'd felt energised and free. Loneliness had come and gone but it wasn't a constant. It was now. And with it had come some introspection. On 5 January, for instance, I wrote:

Time to reflect on stuff which hasn't helped my state of mind. I've realised how much I miss being normal, having a conversation, being able to cuddle someone or to sleep in a bed. I've realised how much weight I've lost, it isn't good at all.

Ordinarily, I was all too aware of how I must look to outsiders after so long living on the streets, but I did occasionally forget. I wrote:

Met my perfect woman on the train on the way back into town . . . Exchanged smiles but then realised I can't do any more than that as I'm Homeless . . . she looked back at me as I got off the train. Grrrrr, never mind.

The first clues that my isolation might be drawing to a close were beginning to form, but my mind was still a maelstrom, my moods

161

intense and changeable, prone to highs and lows. Within hours of lamenting my loneliness, for instance, I was writing as if I was some kind of street SAS commando:

Picked up gammon and mustard flavoured crisps. Yum! And a big bag of cheese Nachos. No money left again, but as [the former SAS commando turned crime writer] *Andy McNab wrote: 'eat when you can, sleep when you can, you never know when you will again'.*

By this point, I had a medium-sized rucksack that ran on wheels. It contained my clothes, books, magazines, some shaving and washing stuff and other bits and pieces. That day, in Romford, it was expanded by another new jacket and scarf that I had found discarded in a wheelie bin. Wearing two jackets had soon become a necessity. The following day, 7 January, I wrote:

This is how cold it is. Trafalgar Square ponds are frozen as are parts of Grand Union and Serpentine.

After eighteen months without any human contact, my craving for some kind of interaction was obvious in my scribbles. My entry for later that same day described how I'd been walking along Oxford Street:

Three girls sat at the bus stop. Oxford Street was closed while they were taking down the Christmas lights, so being the nice guy I told them they needed to walk up to Marble Arch, which two of them did and latched on to me all the way down, which was nice, bit of company for 10 minutes.

The company wasn't always so welcome, of course. While the cold snap continued, I'd spent large parts of my days sleeping on the Underground or on buses. I'd not been as inconspicuous as I would have liked. On 10 January I recorded:

I'm now a statistic on the underground. I'd fallen asleep at the back of the train as usual on the Piccadilly Line, but I'd slumped over onto my knees, a worried passenger had pulled the alarm and I was awoken by the driver and two station staff who thought I'd fainted or passed out. Once on the move again, the driver announced that he was 'sorry for the delay, but it was caused by a passenger being taken ill in the rear carriage who was just asleep'. So I hotfooted away from my embarrassment at Finsbury Park to be greeted with a board that said 'minor delays on the line owing to passenger illness!' Sorry!!!

The 'sorry' typified something that ran through the diary like a seam within a piece of marble. I was living outside society, yet – for whatever reason – I respected its rules. I wouldn't step outside them, and railed against anyone who did. An entry on the 10th about the daily walk along Oxford Street exemplified this:

Have noticed a lot more beggars along the way, which is winding me up. I have never and will never break the law, however these guys do it day in day out, never get arrested, and make more money than me, despite me walking up to 18 hours a day. It's really annoying that honesty doesn't get rewarded.

Reading the diary now, the sense that I was running out of road was tangible. I must have instinctively known it. Something needed to happen. And soon it did.

★

The nine days or so that changed everything began when I woke up on the bench at No 3 Riverside View one morning to find I'd had a visitor. I'd been left all sorts of 'presents' during the past eighteen months. Some were thoughtful – I'd been donated sandwiches, bars of chocolate, blankets, books – but I'd had some unwelcome 'gifts' as well. One joker's idea of a really funny prank was to leave some dog faeces on my blanket. The stench had woken me up early. I'd spent the following day rummaging around for a replacement blanket.

That particular morning, however, it was a business card that had been left for me. I found it resting on my chest. It was embossed with the name of a homeless charity, The Connection at St Martin's. The note simply said: 'Come and see us at our day centre'. The address was near Charing Cross, no more than a couple of hundred yards from No 3.

I was unsure at first. I'd seen assorted outreach workers around, mainly talking to guys who slept rough in the obvious places, in the doorways on the Strand or around Covent Garden. Most of them seemed very decent, committed, caring people. Their hearts were definitely in the right place. They were just trying to do their best for people who had fallen through the cracks. But I tended to ignore them and my natural instinct – at first, anyway – was to treat the invitation the same way. The first clue to my change of heart appeared in my diary on 12 January.

It had begun as a typical day in my grim routine:

Well new week nearly a very bad start to it. The morning began with 6p in pocket and by half 10 I'd worked that up to 16p by way of a few pence here and there and 5p at London Bridge. I hadn't eaten all day and only had a 1/4 of cola from takeaways that I'd found. Picked up a 1/4 bag of soft McCoys and was walking along Oxford Street praying that Romford would come good tonight when I decided to walk down Berwick Street. Now I never go down that way as I've never seen the need, but at the top outside a restaurant I found £1, then at the market another! So although I've hardly eaten (found cold chips in Romford, well a small handful) I've got money to buy supplies tomorrow. I could go now to a 24 hour shop but I'm holding off. I've decided to bite the bullet. I'm going to try St Martins tomorrow and see what's on offer, so there'd be no sense in spending money if I can get Breakfast in there. So we will see what happens.

What happened in the short term was that I discovered getting to St Martin's wasn't as easy as it sounded. The following day, on Tuesday 13 January, I wrote:

I did go to St Martins this morning, however there was a very long queue so will try again tomorrow, get there earlier, right, back later if anything else happens.

The thought of a warm bed or a meal must have taken hold because later that day I wrote another introspective, rather mournful note:

Back again, decided that as Jan has flew by so quickly I'm gonna write a wish list of things I'd like between now and the end of the month and see what happens. 1. Bed for a night. 2. Burger King burger hot or cold 3. Any kind of note, English or foreign 4. Batteries for the MP3, stop me thinking mad things like this! 5. A hot meal ... either Jacket potato with cheese, ham, egg and chips or GBK. Now I know these seem far fetched, however, if I stay positive then it gives me something to hope for!

The following day had delivered some of that hope, but also an episode that summed up my strange relationship with a world I had shunned yet seemed more attuned and empathetic towards than the rest of the population:

I'd walked down from Holborn and turning on to the Strand at Aldwych, I saw a guy on the floor, wrapped around a traffic light out cold. A German man walked past, said 'I think he's dead' and walked off! I got the guy to respond just as a girl from the pub and two mates arrived on the scene. She took over, very demandingly got him to stand up and he staggered a few steps, and threw up! Nice. Well at this point her friends legged it from the scene, to be honest, a very good move, however, I couldn't

165

leave him in the state he was in. After he finished vomiting he took a moment then started to stagger off. This had now been nearly 15 minutes since I'd first come across him. I said good-night to the girl and assured her I'd follow him for a bit to make sure he was okay, didn't want him walking out into the road! He made it as far as Charing Cross Police Station and stopped again so I legged it up to a couple of coppers and handed him over to them. I hope he's okay.

A few hours later, after a sleep at No 3, I was back at Charing Cross. The significance of the step I was about to take wasn't lost on me. Nor were the flaws that had driven me to this point in my life. As I readied myself to re-enter the world, my diary turned intro-spective again:

Well I've done the first step. I'm here outside St Martins. Still got an hour and fifteen minutes before they open but I'm here. I've worked out what my problem is, basically I'm fiercely independent, ever since I started working when I was 16 I've stood on my own two feet. So asking for help isn't something I usually do, which has basically been my downfall. Looking back if I'd accepted the help when it was offered . . . I wouldn't be in this mess, however I prom-ised I wouldn't refer to the past and am going to continue to look forward!

Looking back on it now, I can see that the person who presented himself at St Martin's that day must have been a mess, mentally and physically. I'd not had a proper conversation with anyone in a long time, so the words wouldn't have come easily. My clothes were pretty scruffy and were hanging off me. I had made a point of shav-ing, but my skin and general complexion couldn't have looked great. I'd been out in all weathers for a year and a half. My unease must have been obvious. That day I wrote:

I feel very uncomfortable but will see how it goes. Gotta hang around for some kinda induction, no idea what! Had some toast – 10p a slice. Free tea and coffee.

The good news was that I'd landed in a place filled with professionals used to dealing with broken souls like me. So they weren't fazed in the least. An hour or two into my first visit, I'd felt at ease enough to scribble:

Well it's not too bad so far. Have now had the initial assessment, am now waiting to be seen by another person, they may be in a position to help me with my ID and then potentially benefits. Not gonna get my hopes up, however, defo need to have some money to be here especially for Saturday and a full English! Am gonna try for a shower after I've spoken to the next person, then hit the road, outta money so can't have lunch here.

One of the conversations I had that day touched on the subject of work. I'd been asked about a potential career, something that – I was still in my twenties – was still wide open to me, in my mind, at least. Maybe it was eighteen months listening to radio or maybe it was the performer in me raising his head again, but I told the outreach workers that day I was set on a career in, of all things, broadcasting. I wrote:

The person I spoke to said he was going to try and get me a place volunteering in hospital radio. Which is something I can do whilst being out on the streets and he also thinks I can have a fully funded Radio Producers course. Yippee, things are looking up, potentially, feet are staying on the ground for now. I then had a yummy lunch of jacket wedges and chips and also Iain Duncan Smith from the Conservative party popped in. Randomly.

Back on the streets and locked into my daily routine again that evening, I looked back on a day well spent. I wrote:

Without doubt the best day of the year so far! KFC chips in Leyton, warm chips at TCR, cold chips in Romford, cookies and eclairs (as a treat) from Asda Barking. Finally for the first time in a long time I'm smiling. I can see a tiny chink of light at the end of the tunnel. Still a very long way to go, but it's a very good start.

From then on, St Martin's became a regular haunt for me. I slowly gained the confidence to spend time there. I was still reluctant to mix with others and found ways to entertain myself. On Friday 16 January, for instance, I wrote:

Average day really, went to St Martins, had some toast. Played on keyboard for a while, gonna learn properly at some point.

During those early days, my greatest pleasure was having a decent meal. I'd save up the money I found on the streets to buy toast and – best of all – a breakfast fry-up. I'd resisted the temptation at first, purely on the basis of cost, but on Saturday 17 January I wrote:

I didn't add any money to what I had overnight so got to St Martins with about £1.50. I'd decided that I'd hold off from Breakfast and just have a shower but the smell was too much and I had egg (was given 2 for 1 as they were the last ones!), sausage, and chips with a slice of Bread, all for £1.30.

Life on the street was still unpredictable and dangerous at times. The following Tuesday, 20 January, I returned to the diary after losing my pen:

Saturday, not long after I wrote I got a smack in the face from a random stranger. Tickled me but didn't hurt.

But by the following day I was rejuvenated. Excited, even. On Wednesday 21 January I wrote:

Yes, Yes, Yes! First up I find the one thing that if I was in the real world I'd die to own ... Drum roll please ... an iPhone 3g. Found it in Romford. However my honesty part of me has won over my instinct and I'm going to hand it in! It's the right thing to do and should it not be claimed in four weeks it's mine anyway!

The days when such discoveries kept me going were drawing to a close, however. The signs were plain to see. My focus was increasingly going to be on visiting St Martin's and beginning the long process of rejoining society. It was already underway. Later that same day, I wrote the final few entries in my short-lived chronicle of that month.

Next up ... Benefits, they have to send the forms out to me which isn't a problem should get them in a couple of days, but after a bit of toing and froing I got a crisis loan.

My final comment to my diary hinted at the life that was drawing to an end and the one that was soon to begin.

Got £90ish and treated myself to a Burger King Wishlist. Also got £5 pair of trainers from Asda along with some socks.

It would take time. I had, as I'd already reflected, 'a very long way to go'. But, in my new trainers, I was ready to start the slow walk back into the real world.

11

NATIONAL TREASURE

Who presented the 2002 Brit Awards alongside Frank Skinner?
Jay's Quiz on BBC Radio 2, May 2020

Which movies had the taglines:
– You don't get to 500 million friends
without making a few enemies.
– In space, no one can hear you scream.
Jay's Virtual Pub Quiz No 15, May 2020

What does a red flag in motorsport signify?
Jay's Virtual Pub Quiz No 6, April 2020

It was the eighth Thursday quiz and I had just completed the first round of questions. Outwardly, I was trying my best to pretend it was just another ordinary night, but inside I was giddy with excitement. I took a deep breath and leaned into the sleek new microphone I'd added to my new-look 'studio'.

'And for Round Two,' I said, 'I'm going to hand you over to the national treasure that is Stephen Fry.'

I sat back and shook my head. Ten years earlier I'd been a homeless person, imagining him reading a Harry Potter book to me on the bench on the Embankment. Now the comedian, actor and host of the hugely popular BBC quiz show *QI* was sharing a screen with me, live from his study somewhere in the east of England.

171

'Thank you, Jay. You are a marvel,' he said, before moving seamlessly into his first question: 'Which of America's states comes first alphabetically?'

In the space of a few short weeks, my life had been transformed so completely that events like this had become almost commonplace. Anything could happen now. I simply expected the unexpected.

That day – 14 May 2020 – was a case in point. Even before I handed over to Stephen that night, there had been a succession of 'pinch me' moments.

It had begun early, a little after 8 a.m., with the fulfilment of a dream.

I was stunned when Alex first told me that BBC Radio 2's biggest show had been in contact. Apparently, one of the team on Zoe Ball's breakfast broadcast was a fan. She'd regularly taken part in my Thursday quizzes and had been nagging her colleagues to invite me on. They'd finally agreed. Was I free to appear and maybe ask a few questions?

I initially told myself that it was simply an idea, and it would fall to pieces in the planning stages. The show was listened to by more than seven million. They'd realise their mistake and book someone else. But it never happened and that morning, around 8.15 a.m., I was connected to a BBC link and heard myself talking to Zoe Ball.

It was weird. Back in the 1990s, as a kid, I used to watch her on the TV show *Live & Kicking* with Jamie Theakston, Andi Peters and others on Saturday mornings. Now here I was joshing around with her live on radio. While being listened to by millions of people. I tried not to think about that bit.

Zoe asked me about the surreal turn my life had taken in the past few weeks, then invited me to ask a few questions.

I had put together a mix that I thought would be entertaining. Which is the largest of the Channel Islands? In slang terms, what is the value of a 'monkey'? What is the favourite food of the Teenage Mutant Ninja Turtles? The final question was a bit of a trick one.

The answer – about who presented the 2002 Brit Awards – was actually Zoe herself.

It all went well enough, but afterwards my imposter syndrome was in overdrive again. I was convinced thousands of irate BBC listeners were going to call in, pointing out my answers were wrong. They weren't, unless overnight Guernsey had, in fact, grown bigger than Jersey, and Leonardo, Donatello, Raphael and Michelangelo had recently developed a taste for pasta rather than pizza. So they never came. Instead, Alex and I got an email from an executive producer saying they'd never had such a response to an item.

'It's up to you, but would you be up for doing it again next Thursday morning?' he asked. 'It might even become a regular slot.'

During my darkest days on the Embankment through to my first conversations at The Connection at St Martin's, I'd always dreamed of a career on the radio. And now here I was, not just appearing but potentially having a regular slot on one of the BBC's biggest shows. Several of my friends sent me congratulatory emails. A few of them knew what it meant to me.

If it had been any other day, I would have shut up shop there and then and celebrated. But it wasn't any other day. Nowhere close.

If anything, the other news that morning was even more surreal. An announcement had been released via 10 Downing Street and the office of the Prime Minister. It confirmed the details outlined in the letter I'd received days earlier. When it arrived, with the familiar portcullis motif on the envelope, I at first assumed it was some kind of prank. Someone had photoshopped it. To be honest, I wasn't entirely convinced it was genuine even after reading it. Boris Johnson had, in his own inimitable style, written the letter in the form of a quiz. It read:

Dear Jay

 As you host your latest Virtual Pub Quiz tonight, I wanted to contribute some questions of my own.

Question One: Which quizmaster hosts the biggest online quiz in the world?

Question Two: Which former pub landlord has now raised over £160,000 to support our wonderful NHS?

Question Three: Which great Lancastrian has just won the UK's 1372nd Point of Light award in recognition of his incredible efforts to bring people together from across the world?

The answers are, of course, you!

On behalf of the whole country, and thousands of your participants stretching right across the globe, thank you for lifting our spirits at this time.

And I wish you – and everyone taking part online – another fantastic Virtual Pub Quiz tonight!

It was only after checking with Alex and others that I actually believed it. The Point of Light award was a genuine thing. It was currently being awarded daily and recognised, to quote their official website, 'outstanding individual volunteers – people who are making a change in their community'. When I looked at the previous winners, I saw people who were doing work on everything from improving access to defibrillators to cleaning up plastic waste on our beaches, from giving underprivileged kids experience in the entertainment industry to supporting carers stuck at home looking after loved ones. Three weeks earlier, Captain Tom Moore had been the chosen winner. Now – to my astonishment – it was me.

That morning, I kept rereading the letter. Technically, of course, one of the questions was wrong. I was a Londoner, not a Lancastrian, but it would have been bad form for me to point it out.

I couldn't deny I was chuffed by the recognition. Honoured, even. It wasn't every day the Prime Minister thanked you 'on behalf of the whole country ... for lifting our spirits'. But as my email inbox lit up with requests for interviews and comments from the media that morning, I had precious little time to dwell on that either.

Instead, I had to crack on with getting ready to co-host the quiz that night – with my rather famous new broadcasting partner.

★

Enlisting Alex had turned out to be a masterstroke. Our 'business model' had been evolving just as we'd hoped. On the financial side, Patreon had been a huge boost to my parlous finances. The number of patrons committed to paying monthly had ended at more than four thousand, a mind-bending number. I sensed that a lot of them had made one-off payments and would not become regular monthly funders. But I was fine with that. I was grateful. It would allow me to focus entirely on creating quizzes.

We'd also struck up a good relationship with YouTube and had begun to generate money from ads on our live and pre-recorded quizzes. It wasn't life-changing money, but – added to the Patreon donations – it was enough to ease my worries and for me to be able to put Alex on a retainer. It was the least I could do – he'd been a revelation and had helped me so much.

On top of his other work, he had started negotiations with a publisher to turn my quizzes into books. This was outside even the craziest scenarios I'd imagined for myself on the streets. Me, having my name attached to a book? That was never going to happen in a million years. But within weeks I had a contract and a delivery and publication date with Mirror Books. I was going to be a published author. I was already at work selecting the questions.

What had made me most happy, however, was what Alex had done on the charity front, which was the main reason I'd teamed up with him.

His connections had opened the door to lots of big charities. We'd thought long and hard about which one to make our second, official cause. The Prime Minister's letter had actually understated how much our first fund-raiser, for NHS Charities Together, had pulled in. It was in fact more than £170,000. We knew we could make a huge difference to all sorts of good causes, but eventually settled on Alzheimer's Research. It was an issue that affected millions of families around the country. At the outset, the charity had said they might be able to get some celebrities involved and they'd been as good as their word. Tonight's quiz marked the start of our campaign for them – and Stephen Fry was the first celebrity to come on board.

Truth be told, I'd been wary of teaming up with celebrities or outside corporate interests. I worried whether it fitted in with my image as an ordinary guy with his rather haphazard and accident-prone pub quiz. My greatest fear was that people would think it was all contrived and part of some great master plan. It was a pretty paranoid thought, but I'd always had plenty of those.

Those jitters hadn't been helped by the brief celebrity appearance we'd had two weeks earlier, as we wound up the appeal for the NHS. Following an approach to Alex by someone connected to the Take That singer Gary Barlow, we'd happily welcomed his offer to provide some 'half-time entertainment' on the quiz. I was over the moon that someone so high profile was willing to aid our cause. He was really generous with his time and played a brief medley of songs from his living room, including 'Back for Good' and 'Greatest Day'. I was left dumbstruck as I watched him perform. I never in a million years thought I'd be sharing a screen with someone who was on my playlist when I was on the streets.

But his appearance had turned out to be a little bit divisive. Most of the feedback was positive, but one or two players had made negative comments about the controversy over his politics and tax affairs, something I knew nothing about.

'Whoa. I wanted a quiz, not some jaded, faded Tory tax dodger,' one player had written.

From my point of view, more worrying were the comments made by a couple of other players. 'How to lose all your patreon supporters in one go. Step one: THIS.'

It seemed really unfair, not just on me but on Gary Barlow. What did this have to do with his private financial arrangements? How could people criticise him for supporting the NHS at a time like this?

Fortunately, we experienced none of the same problems with Stephen Fry and his quiz went like a dream that night. He was every inch the professional I'd expected him to be and very generous to me. He referred to me as The Jayster and Prime Minister Quizling. He even called the second of his rounds Geberal Knowledge in a nod to one of my missteps in an earlier quiz, where I'd somehow mangled the word General. I'd made it a regular feature ever since. By the end of the evening, we'd already raised tens of thousands for Alzheimer's Research.

There were two more celebrity appearances in the pipeline before the appeal ended. Jonathan Ross and Scarlett Moffatt were both going to take part. I was confident that we'd beat even the amount we'd raised for the NHS by the end of it.

★

My profile remained sky high in the media. At the end of April, I had done an interview with the *Washington Post*. It had been another 'pinch me' moment. One of the most famous investigative journalism publications in the world wanted to talk to me about how quizzes were keeping the UK population going during lockdown. It was just ridiculous.

The piece was very good. It featured other quizmasters, like Marcus Berkmann, the writer who had switched his regular quiz at the Prince of Wales in Highgate, north London, online, renaming it 'Quiz Night at the Covid Arms'. I liked his line of questions. 'What is wider, Australia or the moon?'

But it also underlined something that had become more and more apparent to me. 'Fans say the events are bringing people together, puncturing the isolation bubble, making dark days a little bit lighter,' wrote the article's author, Karla Adam.

My interactions with my fans had become more and more important. I loved hearing the stories of how people had come together. A favourite was the tale of how a small terrace of houses in the Midlands had begun doing the quiz each Thursday while sitting outside next to the fire pits they lit in their gardens. It had escalated to such an extent that they had somehow rigged up a projector and were beaming the quiz – and my image – onto a large whitewashed wall at the end of their cul-de-sac. I called them the Firepitters. Another team, the Mill Lane Mob, had been very generous in supporting me on Patreon and I'd become friendly with one of their members, Dan, who shared a passion for Formula One. I lived in dread of asking a question on the subject on a Thursday night and having him correct me. A family based in Arizona, in the US, played each week, usually by watching a replay on YouTube. They didn't care that the quiz could be quite UK-centric. If in doubt when an obscure British TV question came up, they simply answered *EastEnders*. Once or twice, they'd actually been right. We'd become friendly and chatted often. They'd already asked me to do a private quiz for them when Christmas came.

It made me feel great to know that I was making things, as the *Washington Post* piece put it, 'a little bit lighter' for people. But for all the highs I was experiencing, there were – inevitably – some lows to go with them. It was in my nature to fret and dwell on them, unfortunately.

I've never been someone to take praise easily and I found the fact that I was 'sort of famous' hard to handle. I didn't mind people stopping or waving at me in Darwen. It didn't happen often, thankfully, but I was polite, always. How could I not be? The chances were that they'd played the quiz at least once. I could only be grateful to them. It could even provide a moment or two of comic relief.

One of my most frequent gaffes as a quizmaster had always been mispronouncing words or names. In one of my early quizzes, I'd asked: 'Emmental is what type of food?' The only problem was, I'd pronounced it Emma Mental. I'd got a fair bit of stick for it, but most people thought it was just funny.

I was in the local supermarket a week or so later when I over-heard a mother and her teenage child in conversation. 'Mum, can we try that Emma Mental cheese?' The mum laughed and replied: 'You only want to try it because of that funny quiz guy.' I just smiled to myself and slipped out of the supermarket as discreetly as I could. I hadn't been quite sure how to react.

But it was the more personal scrutiny and the judgement that people now felt entitled to make that had begun to unsettle me.

Alex and Paige had, since the beginning, done their best to protect me from the worst of the comments that people made online. Especially the personal ones. I'd spot them on Paige's face sometimes as she was monitoring the live comments. She'd frown or growl, then punch away at her laptop, angrily deleting or hiding them from me. But I knew they were out there. And I knew what people were saying. As the quiz grew bigger and bigger, there were times when, inevitably, stuff would slip through the net.

The comments about Gary Barlow's half-time entertainment had bothered me a little bit. Especially the comment about it being a way to lose my Patreon support. I knew the fact I was receiving money now was a sensitive subject. And it wasn't the first comment I'd received since opening the Patreon page. One night, someone had accused me of 'selling out'. Others had made snide comments along the lines of 'you're charging people for this now, you need to brush up your act'. I tried to take it with a pinch of salt, but found it difficult. I was a natural worrier and it had continued to nag away at me ever since.

The other source of criticism had become the so-called 'quiz-master fraternity', other people who ran competitions either in pubs or clubs or even online, up and down the UK and beyond.

I'd read comments saying: 'He's a fraud, he's never hosted a quiz in his life.' 'He's stolen all these questions.' 'He planned this from the beginning.'

Alex would always say 'don't engage'. 'If you engage with them, they win. That's what they want.' But it was hard for me. Especially as I'd tried to be supportive. I put up lists of other quizzes that people could join each week. I didn't know what more I could do. Did they want me to hand my quiz over to them?

At one point, I came across two regular pub quizmasters in a chat room that I had joined way back. 'The whole of the quiz fraternity think he's a disgrace,' one of them wrote. It stopped me in my tracks. A disgrace? What had I done to deserve that? OK, I'd mangled the odd question here and there and misplaced a comma or two. I'd mispronounced the name of a Swiss cheese. Did that make me a disgrace? Really?

I knew that a lot of it boiled down to jealousy. They were regular quizmasters. They clearly had access to the internet. Why hadn't they done what I'd done? Had they thought it was a bad idea? Or beneath them somehow? But it didn't soften the blow and the wound it opened up within me. That word – disgrace – became implanted in my head. I couldn't shake it loose.

As for the suggestion that I'd planned it, that was beyond my comprehension. If I'd really done that, wouldn't I have cashed in after the first quiz? Just put it behind a paywall and made the millions that everyone seemed to think I was making? But I'd deliberately resisted that. Now I began to think that maybe I should have taken the money and run. That I should have cashed in at the outset rather than open myself up to such an unjustified attack. As May continued, I began to worry more and more. I realise now it was a by-product of my exhaustion. I was running myself ragged. When I was doing pre-recorded quizzes, I had to wait until everyone was in bed. There were too many noises, too many doors closing as Sarah and Paige went upstairs. I also needed to concentrate, not be distracted. So I'd sometimes end up in the living room until 4.30 or 5 a.m. I'd be utterly drained by then and I'd know that Jack would be up within an hour or two, expecting me to be a full-on dad and get his breakfast. But I'd press on.

At those moments, I'd be at my most vulnerable. I would see a quote: 'He's useless.' 'He doesn't deserve it.' 'Who does he think he is?' And it would send me diving into a depressive state. Sometimes, my mind would go into overdrive. One night, as I lay wide awake in bed mulling over things, I'd begun to feel that my critics were all gathering together. I began imagining a version of that famous scene from *The Simpsons* where a mob come after Homer while they're trapped inside a dome over Springfield. I saw this crowd of people, wielding pitchforks, baying for me. And the crowd just kept doubling exponentially. Two people, four, eight, sixteen, thirty-two . . . and on and on.

I had never accepted praise. I had always accepted negativity. It was a flaw in me, I knew that. It was heartbreaking that I couldn't fully enjoy what I was doing. And I knew that if I let it build up and get on top of me, it would break me as well.

Part of the problem was that so much of the criticism didn't make any sense. The comments about me being overpaid, for instance, were silly.

I was working sixteen hours a day. Six or sometimes seven days a week. That was 100 hours a week, 400 hours a month. At that rate, once I'd taken out what I paid Alex and others, my hourly rate for doing what I was doing was way below the minimum wage. And yet people resented it.

I didn't know how the idea had even taken root. It wasn't as if I was waving the money I was making in people's faces. I didn't come on each Thursday dressed in flashy designer gear or wearing a heavy bling chain around my neck. I wasn't now broadcasting live from my studio in the Caribbean. I was still coming live from my house, as I had been from the outset. I'd not even bought a new shirt.

My Patreon supporters were very vocal in defending me, but it couldn't stop my mind from tracing a familiar trajectory.

I told myself it was wrong. I needed to focus on the positives, the good things I'd achieved so far. And there were plenty of them. Between the NHS and Alzheimer's Research, I'd raised almost half a million pounds. I'd had a letter from the Prime Minister thanking me, for goodness' sake. I heard my grandad's familiar, soothing voice, repeating all those things. But it's pointless arguing when the loudest voices in your head are drowning out everything else. There's little you can do.

They say the animal instinct within all of us when faced with a crisis is to do one of three things – freeze, fight or take flight. I tended not to be someone who froze; I either fought or took flight. My fear now was that I would succumb to the latter again and do something on the spur of the moment. I might switch on my computer one Thursday night and blurt it out. 'Ladies and gentlemen, thanks very much for all your support these past months, but I regret to say that this is the last edition of Jay's Virtual Pub Quiz. Goodnight and goodbye.'

I knew from my troubled past that I was capable of doing something self-destructive, impetuous – something frankly crazy like that. What I was forgetting, of course, was that this same past had taught me much more than that . . .

12

JAY 2.0

What is the name of the process of growing
things in water without soil?
Quiz 12, Jay's Virtual Pub Quiz Book 2

Which company's slogan is 'impossible is nothing'?
Jay's Virtual Pub Quiz No 19, June 2020

As winter 2009 gave way to spring and the world began to blossom into life once more, I was undergoing a rebirth of my own.

I can look back and almost smile at it now. I picture an almost comic scene from a cheap 1970s sci-fi B-movie. A cross between *Frankenstein* and *The Six Million Dollar Man*. A bedraggled and broken version of myself is wheeled into a laboratory and surrounded by doctors and nurses, technicians equipped with computers, tubes and blinking lights. They fit me with wires and microchips, pieces of computer hardware, download programmes into me. At the end, I emerge from a huge cloud of dry ice, repurposed, rebuilt, ready to resume my place in the world. Jay 2.0.

The reality, of course, was that it was a much more serious, laborious and less dramatic process. In all, it took the best part of nine months for the Connection at St Martin's team to revive and reconstruct the empty husk of a person they had on their hands.

★

Everyone who passed through the big red doors of The Connection building near Charing Cross was treated as an individual. The staff understood that no two homeless people's experiences were identical. The root causes might be the same – addiction, bankruptcy, mental illness, relationship breakdowns – but the paths that led people towards a life on the streets were all unique. They knew that their first job was to make people feel safe. Their 'clients', as we were called, had to believe they were stepping into a refuge, somewhere that offered an escape from their problems, whatever they were. In order to do that, they had to win their trust. For me, someone who had developed huge trust issues, that was the key.

So at first they treated me like every other client and let me take things at my own pace, while I – and they – built up our trust of each other.

It began with routine. Slowly, I started to use more of their facilities to shower, wash my clothes, use the internet or just hang out and grab some decent food. If I knew something particularly tasty was coming up on the menu in their kitchen, I'd save up the money I found on the streets. Jacket potatoes and the weekend breakfast 'fry-up' were always a favourite.

I was assigned a 'key worker', a guy called Adrian, whose job it would be to guide me back into the world. He was a straight shooter. There was no nonsense with him. It was a kind of tough love.

Ironically, he said it would have been easier if I was a drug addict or alcoholic. There were more readily available programmes and funding for treating addictions. There were specialist charities dedicated to providing everything from accommodation to psychotherapy. But as I didn't have those issues, it was going to take longer to work out what I needed and how they were going to help me. Adrian told me: 'We're not going to have you off the streets next week, it could be six months, but we know where you are. We can keep our eye on you, protect you.'

And so, while I continued to sleep at No 3 Riverside View, I was also now beginning to see The Connection centre at Charing Cross as my second home and the staff there as my new family as I visited more regularly.

I got on particularly well with the centre's manager, a guy called Pete Mason. Like me, he was a football fan, and we'd regularly talk about the latest Premier League results or transfer news. He was a fan of Arsenal, my team Spurs' arch-rivals, but I forgave him for it. He had a natural warmth and charisma.

Conversations weren't always easy. Eighteen months without any interaction with others had taken its toll. The garrulous Tigger of a few years ago had become more of an Eeyore. I was downbeat, introverted, cautious. I'd almost retreated into my early childhood self. But, painstakingly, skilfully, Pete and Adrian began to draw me out.

Adrian was surprised, and a little impressed, that I had managed to make my home on a bench on the Embankment. 'Pretty brave place to sleep every night,' he said when we first spoke. He visited me there a couple of times, especially when the weather was bad. He explained that The Connection had an emergency night shelter that they used to house the most vulnerable rough sleepers. 'If you feel like you're in danger or threatened, you might be able to stay there,' he told me. I never took him up on the offer. A part of me remained independent. I still regarded the streets as my main home. Much as I trusted Pete and Adrian and their team, I wasn't quite ready to come in from the cold.

Throughout that spring and early summer I continued to live the same existence, travelling around in search of money and Travelcards, listening to the radio and my MP3 player and doing puzzles in the newspapers I picked up. But during my visits to the centre at Charing Cross, I began to talk about the idea of finding a new home and a job. Of finding my feet back in the world.

I'd explained that returning to my 'home' and my mother wasn't even a consideration. That bridge had been burned. It was a non-starter if I was to get well. So, early on, they had started the process of getting me registered as a homeless person with Westminster City Council. It would open the door for me to become eligible for emergency accommodation and some help in getting myself started again.

To help its clients get jobs, the centre had a programme called Workplace, which gave advice on training schemes, work placements and apprenticeships, everything relating to employment. They even had a room filled with suits and outfits for people to borrow if they were going for an interview. During those first conversations in January I'd mentioned my interest in radio, and they'd begun to research careers on my behalf.

Because they were a charity, however, they were only able to help people with free training courses and job placements. They had found a couple of radio production courses that would have suited me, but they were expensive. They didn't have the money to fund them. They'd asked around for job placements or volunteer roles, too, but had drawn a blank.

The centre was at the heart of the West End; there was a handful of theatres within a stone's throw. I had a little experience in that world from my days back in Wimbledon, but that conjured up bad memories. I didn't feel confident applying for work there, nor at *The Big Issue*, the magazine that offers 'a hand up not a hand out' to people on the margins of society. The team at Workplace said they could get me an interview to become a street vendor, but I just didn't see myself being able to sell anything. It was ironic, I'd been a natural salesman in the past, but – like so much of my personality – that part of me had been hollowed out. My confidence was shot to pieces. I wouldn't have been able to stand on a street corner trying to cajole and charm thousands of disinterested – or, worse, disgusted – Londoners to buy the magazine every day. The rejection that came with it would have been too acute.

So, with Adrian and the team's agreement, I forgot about getting work for a while and focused on getting myself right mentally.

Adrian and I didn't do any therapy or psychoanalysis. It wasn't that kind of relationship. But as I eased back into some form of normality, I found myself, in my own amateurish way, prising open those steel-shuttered doors and finally beginning to take a long, hard look inside myself.

The experience of living on the streets had started the process. It had taught me so much. I'd discovered that I was more resilient than I could ever have imagined. Resourceful, too. As my diary had hinted, I was proud of it. Proud of my independence. But, as I slowly put my toe back in the waters of society, I also saw how bad it had been for me. No man is an island, they say. It wasn't natural to avoid connection and interaction with people, as I had done for so long. It was damaging, in fact. It had made me hollow and, to some extent, dehumanised me. I knew I had to fix that if I was to make a success of my life back in the world.

But in doing that, I also had to correct the other flaws within me. I had plenty of them. They had led me onto the streets in the first place and I knew they could be an obstacle again now as I tried to re-enter the world. I could be impetuous, wilful, self-centred at times. I didn't trust people. It still made me uncomfortable accept- ing other people's help, even at St Martin's where, I knew, people had my best interests at heart. I could work on all of those things, I felt sure. The more I thought about it, the clearer it became. I'd become the person I'd needed to be in order to survive on the street. I must now become the person society needed me to be in order for it to accept me back. Who knew who that person was, what that 'need' was going to be? But if I could find it, I could grow from there. I could become not just Jay 2.0, but 2.1 and 2.2 and more.

Nothing helped me make that transition more than the five-a-side football matches The Connection organised each week. It was Pete who invited me to join them. He knew how keen I was on foot- ball. 'Come along, it'll be fun,' he said.

I'd played a bit of football at school, but I was nowhere near good enough for the first team. We had a player called Leon Britton. He ended up playing Premier League football for Swansea City. I wasn't within a million miles of him.

I hesitated at first. All I could see were the obstacles. I didn't have any kit. Or proper trainers. Where was the pitch and how would I get there? Pete knocked back all my arguments. He said he could get me everything I needed. All I had to do was turn up at The Connection on a Friday afternoon and it would all be taken care of. And so, one Friday late that spring, I turned up at Charing Cross then jumped on a minibus with about a dozen other homeless guys to play in a league based at a pitch over in Russell Square.

I was no Lionel Messi or Cristiano Ronaldo. During that first session I was blowing hard, I was seriously out of condition. But I got stuck in and really enjoyed myself. I was soon joining extra training sessions to prepare us for the league matches. It did me a huge amount of good, not just fitness and strength-wise but in rebuilding my confidence and – little by little – my personality. Traces of the old Tigger began to resurface. 'Typical Arsenal,' I'd tease Pete if he was on the opposite side to me and committed a foul. It was the sort of light-hearted 'banter' you heard on five-a-side pitches everywhere. But, for me, it was priceless interaction. A lifeline. From then on, Friday afternoon was reserved for football. It was locked into my 'diary'. I never missed.

Few things bond people as quickly and effectively as playing a team sport, so fairly soon I had a regular bunch of guys who I knew. The faces weren't always the same, inevitably. People drifted in and out, literally. But it did begin to feel like a community. One with its own rules, its own calendar, its own language. One that I felt a part of. I'd forgotten how important that was. How much we all need that. It was a massive boost.

It's only now, years later, that I can appreciate the cleverness of Pete and the colleague with whom he ran our team, Chris. That was part of their talent, their genius. It was no coincidence that they'd named the charity 'The Connection'. Their job was to reconnect me. Drawing me out onto the football pitch was the perfect way of achieving that. Without me even knowing it was happening.

*

One of the reasons I trusted Adrian, Pete and their colleagues at The Connection was that they kept their promises. That had been a big issue for me in the past. I'd been let down by people too often. If Pete or Adrian said something was going to happen – it happened. And so, almost exactly six months after I'd walked through their doors, in July 2009, Adrian told me that they had found me some temporary accommodation in Leyton, in north-east London. It was nothing fancy and was within a cheap easyHotel where they'd been offered space. The rent would be covered by housing benefit.

I went to see the room. It had a bed, a TV, a shower and a toilet. There were shared cooking facilities within the building. The place's best feature was a lovely rooftop terrace where, after agreeing to move in, I spent a lot of my time. I was so used to being in the outdoors, I had to get out into the fresh air as often as humanly possible.

It wasn't a surprise, I suppose, but I found adjusting to sleeping on a normal bed difficult. For eighteen months, I'd slept on the bench, on Tube trains or on the back seats of buses. It felt unnatural lying on a soft mattress. It was like a scene from one of those movies where a hostage returns to normal life after years in a cell. The first night, I slept in my sleeping bag on the floor. The following two nights, I made it onto the bed but remained in my sleeping bag. It was like a comfort blanket to me.

I was still under the care of The Connection, so I used some of the benefit money I received to buy a bus pass that took me in to central London and Charing Cross. I still did my washing there, used the internet and – in particular – played football on Fridays. That remained sacrosanct to me.

The impact those Friday night kick-arounds had on my rehabilitation cannot be exaggerated. My proudest moment came when, late in the summer, we had one of our regular 'staff v clients' matches. We'd gathered at our usual pitch in Russell Square. Pete grabbed an armband and threw it at me.

'Come on then, Jay, you think you know about the game, let's see how you do,' he said. 'You're captain.'

To others, it may have seemed a minor thing. To me, it was monumental.

For two years, people had barely acknowledged my existence. I was a shadow figure, a non-person on the streets. This person had not only recognised me but was placing his trust in me. I might have been a seven-year-old in the playground again. I was just thrilled to bits.

We had a few decent players, so I shaped the formation of my team carefully. We were younger and fitter than Pete and his team, but they had the experience and the guile. I built our tactics around that, using our speed and stamina to outlast them. It was a close game, but we won 5-2. At the end, I hoisted up the small trophy Pete and Chris had brought along. If I'd been lifting the FA Cup for Spurs at Wembley, I wouldn't have felt any prouder. It was a magic moment for me. And a real turning point. Afterwards, they decided that I was ready to fly the nest, to step free from their protective wings.

As the autumn of 2009 began, they proposed that I take the next step and move into a shared house. Adrian and Pete explained that I would get my own room and that I could furnish and decorate it myself. Effectively, I would be able to set myself up in my own little home. I would no longer be under the protection of The Connection. I would be off their books.

I agreed to give it a go, on one condition – that I remained a member of the Friday night football team. Pete agreed. Adrian told me that I was eligible for a sizeable grant to get started. He gave me the forms and I began filling them in, listing the things I thought I'd need. I'd still not got used to the idea of asking for help, so it was a fairly meagre list. Adrian took one look at it, screwed up the paper and threw it in the bin.

'You should claim for everything you'll need. Pots, pans, knives, forks. Cups and glasses. A toilet brush. You're starting your life over. Try again,' he said in his matter-of-fact way. I'd soon been approved for a grant of almost £3,000, which would be deposited in the bank account The Connection at St Martin's had helped me set up.

A couple of weeks later they took me to a quiet terraced street in Catford, in south-east London. It was not an area I knew particularly well, but that was fine. It felt like a good place to make a fresh start, although, again, I found the adjustment difficult at first. Walking into a supermarket as a 'normal' customer was the strangest experience. I now had a fridge back home and money with which to fill it. But I wandered the aisles of the supermarket almost in a daze, unsure what to do. What to buy? And in what quantities? I came home with a loaf of bread, a packet of frozen chips, butter and a bottle of cordial to make something other than water. And, of course, some custard creams. I was so used to eking out my supplies, I made it all last for a week.

I was careful with my money, drawing it out in small chunks with the cash card I'd been given by the bank. I bought some electrical goods from a second-hand shop – a TV and a digital box, a laptop so I could look for work on the internet and keep up with the news now that I wasn't scouring the streets of London for newspapers every day. I also got myself a cheap phone. Adding my contacts list didn't take long. There was a number for The Connection and that was about it.

I knew I could make the grant I'd been given last for weeks, if not months, if necessary. But I also knew I could take another big step by getting some work. So I began looking for a job, something that involved night shifts if possible. I felt more comfortable with the idea of working when there were few people around. In the meantime, I spent a lot of time exploring my new surroundings in Catford. I'd walk miles, to Bromley in the south, up to Blackheath and Greenwich and the Thames in the north. It was the same routine I'd followed in central London in most respects, except now I had a home to return to at the end of the night.

It took time to settle and one night I found myself so disoriented that I headed up to central London and slept at No 3 Riverside View. It felt odd being back there. I'd moved on, mentally and physically. So having lain there for just a few hours, I was on the first train back to Catford the following morning.

It was now close to a year since I'd woken up on the Embankment with a card in my sleeping bag. The team at The Connection had done so much for me. The debt I owed them was immense. I had no idea how I could pay them back, but that October I had a stab at it by signing up for a charity event, The Tube Challenge. I had to visit every station on the London Underground in under twenty-four hours. It was the sort of thing that appealed to me, and I spent an age planning a route beginning at Terminal 4 at Heathrow on the Piccadilly line and ending at Upminster on the Central line. I even planned the shortest routes through the labyrinth of tunnels that linked different lines together at the key hub stations. I managed it in around eighteen hours and raised £1,500 for them. I made another attempt at it later, on my own, and – briefly – was credited with the fastest time for the Challenge on Wikipedia. But Guinness World Records couldn't verify the time because of a fault on the ticket machine at the start of my attempt. I felt really frustrated. I'd never have another shot at getting in the *Guinness World Records* book, I told myself.

The people I shared the house with tended to keep themselves to themselves, but I began to go out in Catford and slowly made a couple of acquaintances. I got talking to a few women here and there, which gave me some confidence. So then I started dating on an online app. Pretty soon, I became friendly with a really nice lady in Wigan. I travelled up to Lancashire to see her a couple of times, and although we were having good fun together, she soon let me know she wasn't interested in coming down to London. So I began to ask myself: what if I moved up north?

I could make a fresh start. Relocating wasn't going to be a major undertaking. I had two suitcases; that was the extent of my earthly belongings. I had no idea if this relationship had a future, but at least I'd be able to find out and free myself from the burden of the past. No one would know me there. It was a blank canvas.

So I applied for – and got – a job working as a night-shift team leader with Sainsbury's in Wigan. It all happened quite quickly. Sainsbury's were about to enter their busiest time of the year in the run-up to Christmas, so they wanted me to start as soon as possible. Within days, I had handed in my notice at the house in Catford, bought a one-way ticket to Wigan and was preparing to say goodbye to London again.

I hadn't made contact with my mum or my family or any of my friends back in south London and had no intention of doing so now. What was the point? I was leaving again. The only people I felt the need to say goodbye to were the team at St Martin's.

A couple of days before I headed north, I went along for my final Friday football session. I always met the team at Charing Cross and got the minibus with them to wherever we were playing. That day, I arrived early and popped in to see Adrian and one or two of the others who had helped me since my arrival back in January. They were pleased that I'd landed a job and wished me well. Adrian wasn't a demonstrative guy, but he shook my hand. 'You've come a long way, Jay. Well done,' he said.

The football session was fun, as ever, and I couldn't help feeling a little emotional as I said goodbye to the regulars, Chris and Pete in particular. Pete often drove the minibus and he dropped me off back at St Martin's that evening. We joshed with each other along the way. Spurs were due to play Arsenal in a week or so – it was fertile ground for some friendly ribbing. That's exactly what I now considered him to be, a friend.

When we landed back at Charing Cross, I had a shower and handed back my football gear. I offered Pete my hand but instead he pulled me close and gave me a bear hug.

'You know where we are if you need us,' he said.

'I really hope I don't,' I said, trying my best to hold back a tear.

At the time, at least, I meant every word of it.

ROUND FIVE

13

BESIEGED

Music. Yazz said the only way was what?
Quiz 29, Jay's Virtual Pub Quiz Book 1

What was the name of the charity set up because a lady
was too embarrassed to talk about her periods?
Quiz 22, Jay's Virtual Pub Quiz Book 1

I walked into the kitchen, poured myself a large gin and tonic and took a hefty slug.

Sarah was making Jack's supper. She knew me inside out and could tell how anxious I was. She wrapped her arms around me and gave me a hug.

'You'll be fine,' she said. 'People won't think any less of you. You're still Jay.'

I wasn't so sure. All sorts of questions were whizzing around my head. Should I be sharing this with hundreds of thousands of people? Was it going to change people's view of me? Would they even believe me? But I had no option. This was what I needed to do.

I walked upstairs to the spare room and fired up my computer. I switched on the video camera and pressed 'record'.

'Hi everyone, my name is Jay and I'm the host of the Virtual Pub Quiz,' I began. 'About thirteen years ago, I was a homeless person.'

★

I sometimes thought of my mental health as a medieval castle under siege. Most of the time, I'd be secure behind my walls and barricades. Nothing could get to me. I'd feel safe and secure. I'd hold the line. But every now and again, a giant missile would appear out of thin air and slam into me, as if fired by a catapult. When it got really bad, I'd feel like hordes of invaders were scaling the castle's ramparts on ladders, storming the barricades. As May drew on and the quiz became more and more successful, I'd begun to feel that way. It was that mob from *The Simpsons* with the pitchforks again. I was besieged and I was struggling to keep them at bay.

To an outsider looking in, the things that were undermining me would have seemed small. Trivial, even. The hassle and occasional abuse I was getting from other quizmasters was a case in point. I'd done my best. I'd continued to put up lists of other recommended quizzes on cards during my broadcasts. But even that wasn't enough.

'Why was I at the bottom?'

'You spelled my name wrong.'

I'd given a special mention to my fellow publican in Darwen, Leon, who did a quiz called Level 1 that I'd actually taken part in myself online with a few friends. He was a friend too.

'That's favouritism.'

'Why is he getting a special mention?'

It was petty, incredibly so at times. And I knew it.

Sticks and stones may break my bones, but words will never hurt me, my grandad used to say. But it was in my nature to let these things eat away at me. I was helpless in that way. To me, the pen was mightier than the sword.

It was the same with the digs and disparaging remarks. I wished I could let them wash over me, turn a blind eye. But I just found it impossible.

Whenever I read a comment from someone playing the quiz – 'He's just not very professional', 'I don't like his voice', 'His quiz is so dull' – I took it personally.

But the thing that had pushed me to the brink in recent weeks was the way I'd noticed neighbours and friends reacting. I've often heard it said that when someone becomes 'famous', it's not them that change, it's the people around them. I didn't consider myself famous in any way, shape or form, but of course that didn't matter. It was how others saw me that counted. I'd noticed people's attitudes had subtly changed since I'd launched my Patreon and been joined by celebrities on the quiz. At first, I brushed it off. I knew I was prone to overanalysing everything. I told myself I was reading too much into some of the looks I received when I was out and about in the supermarket. It was different to the straightforward thumbs-ups and 'well dones' I'd got when I started back in March. There was a coolness, a standoffishness now.

Of course, there were possible explanations. Lockdown had been going on for weeks now. People were fed up, frustrated, desperate for the world to open up again. Spirits were low. And besides, I was just another local, getting on with his life. Why would they treat me any differently? But my instincts told me that people were judging me a little bit more. I felt sure I'd seen disapproval in some people's eyes. I could almost hear them saying: 'Look at him, Mr Big Shot quizmaster. Earning big bucks now while the rest of us are locked inside our homes.' It started to make me feel really uncomfortable.

Sarah, of course, had told me that I was being silly, that I was imagining it. But then I heard something that confirmed my fears. I was on the phone with a friend one day when he told me. Another member of my social circle, a former colleague in the motor trade with whom, I thought, I'd remained friends, had been bad-mouthing me. 'He's going around saying that you're too high and mighty to even talk to us now,' my friend explained. '"Oh, Jay's worth three-quarters of a million quid, he's too rich and famous to bother with the likes of us any more." I told him it was rubbish, but he wasn't having it.'

I was devastated.

I'd tried to stay in touch with my inner circle as best I could. If I saw Haydn, Gareth, Roy, Ryan, Ste or Sal's name flash up on my phone, I'd always try to take the call, even if it was just to say I'd have to call them back because I was so busy. I'd happily have gone for a couple of pints with them if we'd been allowed to. It would have been just what the doctor ordered, truth be told. But we were still in lockdown.

The accusation also hurt because – deep down – I knew there was a grain of truth in it. I had been totally wrapped up in my new world. I'd been working sixteen hours a day sometimes. I barely had time for Sarah and Jack, let alone anyone else.

But it was his comment about me suddenly being rich that really threw me. Three-quarters of a million? Where on earth had he got hold of that figure?

I googled 'Jay Flynn net worth' and found one of those silly sites that estimate people's supposed wealth. They were notoriously unreliable and inaccurate. I just laughed. It had me down as being worth between $100,000 and $500,000. It wasn't even remotely close. I didn't have £10,000 in the bank, let alone $100,000.

It settled in my head and began to stew away, growing noisier and noisier. It wouldn't just have been that one person who thought this. Those looks I'd received in Darwen – that's what they were about too. Who knew how many people believed the trolls and the critics? As it all began to weigh down on me, the questions kept coming. Were my critics right? Did I deserve this success? Was I some kind of fraud? And if so, was I doing the right thing in continuing? The familiar downward spiral began. Why was I even subjecting myself to all this? What was the point? Wouldn't it be wiser to call it quits before I inflicted some serious harm on myself? Once more, I began to feel overwhelmed. I couldn't see the wood for the trees.

★

The irony was that the quiz had continued to go from strength to strength. More than a hundred thousand people were tuning in with their teams each week and – best of all – our charity efforts were a runaway success. The Alzheimer's appeal had raised more than £200,000 and we were confident we'd reach £300,000 when the shutters finally came down after Jonathan Ross and Scarlett Moffatt had done their 'takeovers'. Along with Alex, I'd already begun to think about the next charity partnership, and the more I thought about it, the more I appreciated that I had to choose wisely. It might be my last fundraiser. My last chance to make a difference. That was a serious possibility, and not just because I might walk away. There were also rumblings now of lockdown being lifted in June. People would soon be freed after three months of incarceration at home. Who would want to sit down and do an online quiz when the world, and more to the point, their local pub was reopened? That was one of the easiest answers ever. Precisely no one.

In light of this, it was important to make sure the next good cause was an especially deserving one. I had worked with big, national charities but I felt I should support something more modest, more down-to-earth maybe. I began to think about working with a charity closer to home. If not in Darwen, then perhaps in Lancashire or the north of England. A local hospice, perhaps? Something dedicated to the local environment? I ran through lots of possibilities. I began to feel it should be something more personal, more relevant to me and the family. Maybe something to do with Sarah's condition, narcolepsy? Or a charity to help the children's wards in the area's hospitals? Jack had benefited from their care when he was first born.

It was while I was listening to the news on the radio one evening that it hit me. I heard an item on how the pandemic had impacted the homeless. It was something that had crossed my mind a couple of times early on after lockdown was declared, for obvious reasons. How were rough sleepers coping? How would I have fared if it had happened when I was sleeping on the bench at the Embankment? But since the quiz had taken off, I'd not had the headspace to give it any more thought. Listening more carefully now, I heard someone talking about how they were relying more and more on the specialist charities that protected and re-homed rough sleepers. I sat bolt upright in my chair. It was blindingly obvious. In fact, I had been stupid not to have seen it before.

'You know where we are.'

I just hoped they were still there.

★

I'd not had any contact with The Connection at St Martin's since leaving eleven years earlier, so it was an anxious moment when I looked them up online. Did they still exist? To my relief, I saw they were still active. I sent an email, which didn't get a reply that day. So the following morning I picked up the phone and called their main switchboard.

It took a while to answer, which didn't surprise me. They must have had a skeleton staff at work.

'Could I speak to Pete Mason, please?' I said when I eventually got through, fully expecting to be told he'd long since moved on.

'He's not here right now. But he'll be back later. Can I say who's calling?'

Later that afternoon, I sat down for a Zoom call on my laptop. Neither of us could quite believe it when we switched on our cameras and saw each other's blurry outlines filling our screens.

'Jay, is that you?' he said.

'How you doing, Pete?' I replied. 'You haven't changed a bit, man.'

It was true. He'd barely aged a day.

What's that old saying about true friends? No matter how long you've been apart, when you meet again it's as if you're just picking up the conversation where you left off. That's the way it was for the next twenty minutes as we caught up.

Pete confirmed what I'd seen on the news: that there were still people on the streets during the pandemic. The government had made an effort to bring them in but – inevitably – some had fallen through the cracks.

'I've got thirty clients in a hotel in Bayswater. I'm giving them breakfast and lunch and laundry facilities. We've had to do a lot of it from scratch,' he said.

It sounded as if he was fighting an uphill battle. It made my next step even more obvious.

'I never felt like I'd said thank you for all you did for me. Not properly anyway,' I said.

Pete remembered the Tube Challenge I'd attempted.

'Nah. You raised a lot of money. You did really well,' he said.

'I might be able to raise a lot more,' I replied. 'Things have changed a bit since then.'

Pete hadn't heard about my success with the quiz. He kept punching the air and whooping when I explained to him what I'd achieved.

'That's amazing. You always were a grafter,' he said. 'You deserve everything that's coming your way.'

He was speechless when I said we'd raised close to half a million pounds for charities. 'And now I'd like to do that for you guys.'

The more we talked, the more obvious it was that I was doing the right thing. I couldn't believe it had taken so long for me to see it. This was something that I really believed in. Something I stood for.

I got Alex and the management team at The Connection involved and we started mapping out what we could do to help. The Connection agreed to provide us with some video footage to promote and explain their work. Someone also suggested we do a video in which Pete and I spoke about my experience and how they had played such a key role in helping me to turn my life around. I was excited and energised. The joy I'd felt during the opening weeks of the quiz began to return. I began to see a way out of the woods.

All this did present me with a problem, however. If I wanted to show people what I stood for, I would need to show them who I was. Who I really was. I had to tell my audience about my own experience of homelessness, about my two years as a non-person on the streets and then about the miracle that had occurred behind those red doors at Charing Cross.

It was a big step to take. Alex and the team at St Martin's agreed it was a good idea, but understood that I had to be careful. I didn't want to open Pandora's box and let loose a lot of bad memories. I should think about it before diving in.

As I mulled it over, I raked over the pros and cons. On the positive side, it was an opportunity to explain homelessness. It's a subject that's so little understood and yet so stigmatised. It triggers all sorts of images and opinions in people's minds. Most people are sympathetic. A lot are curious and ask you to tell them more. They want to understand. They appreciate that we're all capable of ending up in that situation: 'There but for the grace of God go I.' But there are others who are repelled. They associate homelessness with drink and drug abuse. With crime. In some cases, people are completely unsympathetic: 'They just need to do a day's work.' By telling my story, I could potentially make people rethink that attitude.

Of course, the flip side of this was that it would give my critics even more of an opportunity to judge me. It would be ammunition for the trolls and keyboard warriors who seemed to revel in taking a pop at me. Did I want to hand out the bullets for my own execution? I was being too dramatic, I knew, but that was the way my mind worked when it went into overdrive.

There was also the impact it would have on my friends and family.

In the years since I'd moved up north from London, I'd told very few people about that period of my life. I'd certainly not broadcast it at work or in the pub. It wasn't so much that I was ashamed of it. That time had passed. I'd begun to see how it had made me a stronger and more resilient person. It was more that I didn't want to be defined by it. I didn't want it to be a millstone around my neck.

It was as if I was back at The Connection at St Martin's in the winter and spring of 2009, putting the pieces of a jigsaw together again. So I turned back to that time, to see if it could help. I thought it might shake loose a few memories. Provide a couple of answers.

It did much more than that.

I'd kept my old diary from January 2009 in a 'memory box' that I'd put together at St Martin's all those years earlier. It had been part of my rehabilitation, an acknowledgement of that time and what I'd been through. It was still there with my old rucksack and a few other odds and ends. Leafing through the diary, I found that entry I'd scribbled in January 2009, at a low ebb. 'I've realised how much I miss being normal, having a conversation, being able to cuddle someone.'

It reminded me of something. I couldn't quite put my finger on it. I switched on my computer and trawled through some emails. Sure enough, I found a message I'd received from a mother, only a week or two previously. 'My children are both overseas. My son is in America and my daughter in Germany. But every week we get together to do the quiz. It's a lifeline for me. Helps me feel like I'm being normal, having a conversation, while I'm not able to cuddle my kids.'

It spurred another thought. I noticed how often in my diary I referred to listening to Chris Moyles. 'Gonna crack on and listen to Moyles.' 'Listened to the rest of Moyles.' 'Listening to Moyles marathon on Radio 1.' I remembered how I'd always felt that he was talking directly to me. That it was just the two of us. That sparked a memory of another message I'd received in the past month.

'I feel like it's just you talking to me, Jay. You're like a friend to me,' a quizzer in Scotland had written to me.

A switch tripped inside me. How could I not have seen it until now?

Their weekly appointment with me had become a fixed point in people's lives. At a time when very little else was certain, I was something they could rely on. Even more importantly, for some I was the sole voice they heard talking directly to them each week. I was their lifeline, their friend. I was their Thursday night Moyles.

I remembered Sarah and the ninety-two-year-old whose weeks revolved around the conversation he had with his cleaner. It was the same with me and many of those who played the quiz.

What on earth had I been thinking when I imagined throwing in the towel? I'd seen at first hand the damage wrought by isolation and a lack of human interaction. How could I cut those people off? How could I sever their link? How could I risk setting them on the path to becoming that empty shell of a person I'd been when I walked into St Martin's? The answer was obvious. I couldn't. Suddenly, I couldn't just see the way out of the woods. I was running free, in the clearing.

*

At the beginning of the week leading up to the ninth quiz, Peter and I filmed a conversation. To my amazement, he had managed to dig out some footage from our old Friday night football sessions. I looked at an image of myself and couldn't help wondering who that person was. I looked drawn, pale, emaciated. There was a blankness to my stare. I'd come so far. Later that evening, I sat down to make my own video. To explain why I had chosen to support The Connection. But also to get my story out there. To come clean, in a way. My gin and tonic by my side, I carefully, nervously but determinedly, began filming it.

'About thirteen years ago, I was a homeless person,' I began. 'I didn't have a drug problem, I didn't have an alcohol problem. I had just fallen through the cracks, had a few bad times.'

The nerves I'd felt began to ease quite quickly.

'When you find yourself in this kind of trouble, there isn't a rule book that says "congratulations, you're now homeless, these are the steps you take". There's nothing like that. I'm quite proud I never broke the law. I wasn't begging on street corners, I wasn't asking anyone for help.'

I explained how I'd ended up at The Connection at St Martin's. How they'd found me at No 3 Riverside View.

BESIEGED

'Someone from St Martin's happened to find me sleeping there one night. They were quite surprised – they never really thought to look down there because it's the most open, exposed part of London you could possibly find,' I said.

I explained that my goal in supporting them now was twofold. 'St Martin's found me and they put me back on the right path. They're an incredible charity and I really want to help them and repay them for everything they did for me,' I said. 'But I also want to get rid of the stigma that surrounds homelessness.'

I knew my contribution would be complemented by clips of current and past clients talking about what St Martin's had done for them. I didn't need to go overboard. This seemed enough.

I edited and re-recorded it a couple of times, trying to get the tone and the message right. I'd soon come up with a short, eight-minute video, which I posted on Facebook to get things underway. It had been viewed several thousand times by the launch of the official partnership with The Connection on the Thursday night of 28 May.

★

I began the quiz that night with the short film that The Connection at St Martin's had made. The guy who narrated the opening could have been me thirteen years earlier. His voice was gravelly, tired. Devoid of hope. As bleak as the grainy footage of London's empty streets that was accompanying his voiceover on the video.

'I had nothing, I knew nobody,' it began. 'I was a person with no identity.'

As the comments section scrolled down on my screen, I was dreading some kind of negativity. And of course there was some. 'I wonder how many more amateur mistakes he will make tonight,' someone wrote within moments of the quiz starting. But after that, there was nothing. Aside from a few 'well done Jays' and messages saying 'we're behind you mate' or 'great cause'.

It was exactly what I needed to hear. Or not hear, more to the point. By the end of the first night, we'd already raised more than

£15,000 for The Connection. It was a small charity. I knew that money would really make a difference. I knew from personal experience that it might fund someone in a new home or halfway house. It might buy them that loaf of bread, packet of frozen chips and packet of custard creams as they did their first supermarket shop. Or it might pay the salary of another Pete or Adrian. And it might be that they would go on to find another broken soul sleeping on a bench in an unlikely corner of London.

It was a great start. I hoped to raise much more for them over the coming week. It would never repay the debt I owed to them, of course. It was incalculable. In fact, my bill was rising even now.

As I sat under the stars in the garden once more that night, it struck me that they'd ridden to my rescue for the second time. I'd really been struggling to see the way forward. There had been nights when I'd come perilously close to posting a video, a Facebook post or a tweet announcing I was quitting. They'd not only given me a reason to carry on fundraising, they'd led me to a moment of revelation. Way back, during my time at St Martin's, I'd thought about what society needed me to be. This was it. This was why I was doing what I was doing. And why I couldn't possibly let people down by giving it up. How on earth could I pay them back for that? That really was a mission impossible.

Looking up at the stars, I could feel the siege lifting within me. 'I think it's going to be OK, Grandad,' I said to myself.

The brickbats and criticism would still come, of course they would. It was human nature. I'd seen it on the streets. The good and the bad. I'd experience it for as long as I remained in the public eye. The difference now was that I wasn't going to let it get to me any more. I'd answered the questions I'd needed to answer within myself. I knew what I was doing and why. Most importantly, I knew who I was doing it for. It was for Pete and his colleagues at that familiar centre in Charing Cross. It was for the other charities I'd helped and intended to help in the days, weeks, months – and who knew? – years ahead. It was, of course, for Sarah and Jack, but it was also for all the others who, I'd come to realise, were depending on me. They were the people I had connected with. And they were the people I cared about now. As long as there was one person out there who regarded my voice as that of a friend, as some kind of Samaritan, I'd carry on. As long as there was one person for whom I was their connection to the outside world, I'd be there every Thursday.

The invaders could besiege me all they liked, hurl all the missiles they wanted. They weren't going to breach my barricades. They might as well throw those pitchforks away.

14

UNANSWERED QUESTIONS

Who was the Roman god of love?
Jay's Virtual Pub Quiz No 36, August 2020

Captives who show empathy for their captors are
known to be suffering from which syndrome?
Quiz 20, Jay's Virtual Pub Quiz Book 2

In which children's TV show did a boy have
a watch that could stop time?
Quiz 35, Jay's Virtual Pub Quiz Book 1

If you're really lucky, there will be maybe one moment in your life when you realise you are the right person in the right place at the right time. I'm a fortunate man indeed, because it's happened to me twice. In March 2020, but before that, exactly seven years earlier in March 2016. It was then that I'd met and fallen in love with Sarah.

Finding the right person in life is all about serendipity, good fortune. Timing. Some people just put it down to coincidence. From the moment we got together, Sarah and I put it down to fate. We were both meant to be in the same place at the same time.

That place was an online dating site where Sarah had just signed up. It wasn't one of the bigger, better-known ones, which was why she'd joined. In her words: 'There weren't so many weirdos on that one.' I'd apparently been the first message she'd received on the very first day of her membership. She'd obviously decided I wasn't a 'weirdo' and engaged with me.

After a few more exchanges on the site, we'd swapped phone numbers and begun texting each other. Something just clicked. We made each other laugh and found talking – even online – effortless. We were soon pinging notes back and forth dozens of times a day. It got quite ridiculous at one point – we were texting each other all day when we were both at work. My friends later told me that I had a big grin on my face whenever my phone pinged. We carried on like this for three weeks and eventually agreed to meet. Sarah was – quite rightly – cautious, so we chose a public place, under the main clock at Bolton railway station. It was almost halfway between our two homes – I was still living and working in Wigan, while she was in Darwen.

I recognised her from her profile photo when she got off the train and walked along the platform opposite, so by the time she arrived at the clock tower, I was ready. Our conversations had been so natural and easy, it felt like we knew each other already, so I gave her a kiss and offered her my hand. She accepted and we walked off on our first date, chatting as if we'd been seeing each other for months. That first night we barely paused for breath, we spoke so much. I knew, even then, that I'd met the person I'd been looking for, the missing piece in the jigsaw of my life.

We wandered around Bolton, popping into a couple of bars and grabbing something to eat. But the location was all a bit of a blur, we were just so wrapped up in each other's company. I don't think either of us could quite believe how easy it was.

Just how relaxed I was became apparent a couple of hours into the evening. Sarah, it was already clear to me, was someone who wore her heart on her sleeve. She didn't have much of a filter and I really liked her for it. She told me she'd had a bad run with men and had begun to ask herself whether there was anyone out there for her. She was also honest and told me about her medical condition, narcolepsy with cataplexy, which she'd first been diagnosed with when she was just fourteen years old and for which she'd been taking medication three times a day ever since. I'd heard of narcolepsy and knew sufferers fell asleep, but I didn't really understand cataplexy. She explained to me that it was a related condition that caused muscle seizures in situations where she got stressed or overexcited. It meant that she couldn't drive or do anything dangerous in case she had a seizure and jeopardised herself or others. 'It really cheeses me off because I wanted to be a mounted policewoman,' she joked. I really admired her honesty, and so, without really thinking about it in advance, I began to tell her my story. My real story.

My time on the streets of London wasn't something I talked about at that point in my life. As far as I was concerned, it was consigned to the past. That part of my story was over. I didn't want it to define me or be this albatross that I had permanently wrapped around my neck. It would only allow people to judge me, for good or bad. But I also didn't want to use those two years to gain sympathy. That really wasn't in my make-up. With Sarah, all those concerns just disappeared. I just told her, straight off the bat.

She listened intently as I recalled my time at No 3 Riverside View. I was a little nervous at the way she fell quiet. She'd been so chatty until that point. A little voice in my head was asking: have you blown it? I needn't have worried.

When I'd finished, she told me that it didn't make any difference to her what I'd done in the past. Everyone has a past, she said. It was the present and the future that mattered.

'If anything, it makes me admire you a bit more,' she said. 'If you were on the streets that long, it's amazing you didn't turn to drink or drugs. Incredible, really.'

It just reinforced my feeling that this was it. I'd finally found the person with whom to share the rest of my life.

It was all a whirlwind from then on. I was constantly sending her cards and flowers. Her colleagues were gobsmacked at how many roses and bouquets arrived at her workplace. 'Does this guy own a flower shop?' asked one workmate, half joking.

Everything was heading in the right direction, but I had to pass one test, Sarah told me. I had to travel down to Perranporth in Cornwall to meet her favourite aunt, June. If I passed 'the Aunt June test', then all was well. You might say I passed with flying colours. I'd never flown at that point in my life, despite my love of aeroplanes and everything to do with aviation. Not only did Sarah buy us tickets to fly from Liverpool to Newquay, she surprised me by giving me a flying lesson while we were in Cornwall. I went up in a tiny Cessna plane and looked down on the spectacular coastline from thousands of feet in the air. It was one of the most exhilarating experiences of my life. I was on a high throughout our visit. Charming Aunt June proved a piece of cake.

By May that year, we were engaged. For a while, I continued to live in Wigan and we travelled back and forth, but it wasn't long before I'd found a new job and moved to Darwen to live with Sarah. Again, we slipped into the routine easily, as if we'd known each other all our lives. Her condition had frightened me a little at first, but she'd guided me through it and I'd got used to it. Sometimes she'd have episodes that passed so quickly, no one even knew they'd happened. The worst was when she had a cataplexy attack while getting out of the bath at home. The condition means her whole body experiences muscle paralysis, so it had been quite scary. After that, she wasn't allowed to have a bath without me in the house in case it happened again.

Throughout this time, we were scrimping and saving to have our wedding and by July 2016 we had enough set aside. It was worth the wait because – to us – the day was perfection.

We hired a lovely hotel on a golf course in the middle of nowhere in the Lancastrian countryside and invited Sarah's family and my friends from the motor trade in Wigan and Darwen. I'd still not resumed contact with my mum or anyone else back in London and I didn't want it casting a cloud over our day. It was too complicated. Too volatile, potentially. Sarah had understood and supported my decision.

15

ROLE MODEL

Who said: No great discovery was ever made without a bold guess?
Jay's Virtual Pub Quiz No 13, April 2020

At 7.41 p.m. on 16 September 2020, a *ping* alerted me to the fact that an email had landed in my inbox. I sighed. It wasn't great timing. I was at my desk, making final preparations for the latest Thursday night quiz, due to start in four minutes. I told myself I'd better quickly check it nevertheless. Just in case the email had any bearing on tonight.

It was from an unfamiliar and odd-looking address: covid19hon-ourslist@cabinetoffice.gov.uk. It had got past my security and spam filters so I figured it must be safe to open it, at least. If there were any dodgy links or requests, I'd dump it straight into my bin.

The email was headed: 'In Confidence – Letter from the Cabinet Office' and began 'Dear Mr Flynn, Please find an important letter regarding The Queen's Birthday 2020 Honours List attached to this email.'

'What the . . .?'

I looked at the clock, flustered. I now had two minutes to compose myself and start the quiz, but my mind was racing. What was the Cabinet Office doing contacting me? Did they want me to nominate someone for the Honours List or act as a referee maybe? Was the email even legitimate? Was it some kind of trick? I wasn't going to fall for another one of those, I told myself.

A fortnight earlier, Alex had revealed he'd been having

conversations with the Football Association for me to do a mini quiz with the England men's football team. I'd been too excited to wonder why I hadn't been copied in as usual on any of the emails planning the event. When I'd switched on the live link, I was like a kid at Christmas when I saw that the two players they'd selected had strong Spurs links – our current player Eric Dier, and Kyle Walker, our former full back who was now starring for Manchester City. I was a little tongue-tied as I asked them five questions.

I'd just finished the answers, and declared Eric the winner, when the trap was sprung. To my bewilderment, Eric and Kyle said they were inducting me into a very exclusive squad of twenty-three 'players' known as the England Lionhearts, each of whom was being recognised for their work during the pandemic. I was still processing what they were saying when, out of nowhere, Sarah appeared with a framed England shirt with my number – No 23 – and my name on the back. The Football Association had – with the co-operation of Alex, Sarah and her mum – organised sending the shirt secretly to me in Darwen. It had remained hidden in Sarah's mum's house for a week, apparently.

I was a gibbering wreck. I did well to fend off the tears.

Kyle and Eric went on to explain that I was in illustrious company. The No 1 shirt had been awarded to Captain Tom Moore. The No 10 shirt to Joe Wicks. They promised me that, when the COVID restrictions were less stringent, I'd be invited to Wembley for an international match.

It had been a wonderful experience, but it had made me wary. Once bitten, twice shy, and all that. Hence my scepticism about the strange early-evening email claiming to be from the Cabinet Office.

It was only later that night, after winding up the quiz, that I got back to it. I opened up the attachment. The letter was definitely from the Cabinet Office, but it was written in such convoluted and legal terms that I had to read it a couple of times. It began: 'The Prime Minister has asked me to inform you, in strict confidence, that having accepted the advice of the Main Honours Committee, he is recommending that Her Majesty The Queen may be graciously pleased to give informed approval that you be appointed a Member of the Order of the British Empire in the BD2020 Honours List.' Sarah was getting ready for bed, but I called her down.

'Please tell me this is what I think it is,' I said.

She quickly scanned the letter – then just let out a little scream.

'Oh my God, Jay. You've been nominated for an MBE.'

I read the letter again. Hilariously – as far as I was concerned, at least – it had a sentence that read 'the Prime Minister would be glad to know that this would be agreeable to you'. There was a form with two boxes at the bottom for me to confirm this. Yes or No. *Why on earth would they need to ask?* I said to myself, shaking my head. But I guessed there were people who wouldn't accept such an honour, for political or other reasons. I wasn't one of them.

There was a lot more red tape and detail in the letter. It said there would be an official ceremony at some point but 'given the current social distancing measures and restrictions on large events, investitures are not currently taking place'.

By the time I went to bed, I'd read and reread the letter a dozen times, in particular a paragraph at the end. 'There is a clear expectation that those invited to receive an honour are, and will continue to be, role models. Recipients of honours should be aware that membership can be forfeited for a variety of reasons, including criminal conviction and bringing the Order into disrepute.'

Role model? Was that what I was now? And how did that mean I had to behave from now on?

I barely slept that night, my mind turning over all sorts of thoughts, imagining all sorts of scenarios, asking myself all manner of questions. Was I actually going to go inside Buckingham Palace? Was I going to meet The Queen? But would I get that far? Who would be monitoring me to make sure I didn't 'bring the Order into disrepute'?

For the next few weeks Sarah and I kept the news to ourselves, as we had been instructed, which we both found incredibly difficult. Sarah was bursting to tell her mother and family. So it was a huge relief when, in mid-October, the Honours list was formally announced in *The London Gazette* and printed in the press.

I bought myself a copy of a newspaper, just to confirm I wasn't dreaming. I looked down the list of honourees and shook my head in a new wave of disbelief.

The list was heavily skewed towards those who had helped out during the worst of the pandemic. There were senior consultants and nursing officers from hospitals across the country, executives and scientists from the leading pharmaceutical companies. There were logistics managers from the supermarket chains, teachers, senior fire officers, a professor of infectious disease modelling. The list went on and on. And then there was – me. For doing what? Running a quiz that kept people from going stir-crazy? It was the stuff of fantasy. As if we'd entered an upside-down world. Of course, that's what I was forgetting. That's precisely where we'd been, and, to an extent, were still.

Having the news out in the open was a relief, however. The letter in September had made clear that 'once we have received your form we will not need to contact you unless further information is required', adding that the 'Central Chancery will be in touch when it is possible to give you more information about receiving your award'.

That meant I was free to get on with life and the job that had earned me the honour.

★

As 2020 drew to a close, I was grateful – not to mention a little amazed – that it was still a job. Lockdown had been eased across the UK in the summer and I'd fully expected it to signal the beginning of the end of my quiz. But it hadn't worked out that way. I'd been told in no uncertain terms by my most loyal followers that I had to carry on. By the autumn and early winter, tens of thousands were still logging in each Thursday to hear me read fifty questions. I'd actually lost count of the precise figure, but I knew I'd hosted dozens of live events and pre-recorded dozens more speciality ones. My

Patreon support remained loyal too.

Since the 'wobble' I'd had back in May prior to the campaign to raise money for The Connection at St Martin's, I'd adopted a much more philosophical approach to running the quiz. The odd criticism I got was now water off a duck's back. I'd learned to just shut it out. I knew my twice-weekly competition was helping a lot of vulnerable, isolated and lonely people all over the world. And I definitely knew it was doing some good for charities. We had, in the end, raised £90,000 for The Connection at St Martin's. And by the end of 2020 I was immensely proud to have raised more than £1.4 million in all for assorted charities, including Refuge, a charity protecting women and children suffering domestic abuse, Dogs Trust, Samaritans, Barnardo's, the Stroke Association, the RNLI and Air Ambulance and, as a nod towards Alex's amazing contribution to my success, The Diana Award.

My new mindset had also helped me to appreciate how well received my work had been. A while back I'd have been unwilling to take the praise, but as news organisations began doing their round-ups of what had been an extraordinary and difficult year, I felt more and more proud of what I'd done. One news show had done a feature on the so-called heroes of lockdown. They ranged from the pharmaceutical geniuses who were already working on a vaccine to the frontline doctors and nurses who had risked – and in some cases, sacrificed – their lives to save others. Captain Tom Moore and Joe Wicks were inevitably in there, as – to my amazement – was I. 'Jay Flynn is to the nation's mental health what Captain Tom is to fundraising and Joe Wicks is to the nation's fitness,' the reporter said. It meant the world to me.

It wasn't all serious, of course. I was still managing to have some fun. My appearances on Zoe Ball's show on Radio 2 had – as I'd hoped – become a regular feature. I looked forward to joining her live on air after 8 a.m. each Thursday morning and loved the banter she had with her 'crew' of producers and co-presenters. I'd also made a couple of TV appearances, the most exciting of which was on the quiz show *Eggheads*, to mark its move to Channel 5. I'd been asked to compete with my own team and had invited a couple of friends from Darwen down to join me. I'd included an old friend and colleague from the motor trade, Rebecca or Bek, who, since the late summer, had been helping me with my social media. She was an absolute star and had really raised our game on Facebook and Twitter. It was a thrill to sit in a TV studio with people I'd been used to seeing once a week in the pub. My only disappointment was that we didn't win.

Sarah was still my number one supporter and at times got more excited than me about the life I was now living. One of the funniest moments had come one lunchtime when she popped into my office to check up on me. She'd found me talking to someone on a Zoom call and – as she was prone to do – stuck her head in to say 'hello'.

When the figure at the other end replied with 'Oh, hello', she screamed so loudly it was probably heard in his garden, a couple of hundred miles away in Surrey.

'Oh my God, Jay, it's Rick Astley,' she said, as if I didn't know who I was talking to. 'I know, Sarah,' I replied. 'He's going to sing a song on the quiz for us.'

She'd not got over it for days. 'I can't believe it,' she kept muttering. She kept laughing to herself then breaking into a chorus of 'Never Gonna Give You Up'.

★

A few months into 2021, I got a new letter from the Cabinet Office. The COVID situation had eased a little but there was still no plan for a formal investiture, so they were offering me some options. I could accept my award up here in Lancashire and be invited to a Buckingham Palace garden party at a later date. Alternatively, I could have the award posted to me. I wasn't interested in either. I let them know that I would take the third option and bide my time until they could hold an official investiture wherever and whenever it might be. I'd waited the best part of forty years to achieve something in my life. I could remain patient for a few months, or even longer.

There was still plenty to keep me occupied. I had written a

second quiz book with Mirror Books and it was due to be published that November, in time for Christmas. As well as running the regular online quizzes, I'd been approached to do some 'live' competitions for corporate clients. I had also agreed to do a couple of live quizzes for our regular players. The world was beginning to look like a normal place again.

After months of playing to empty grounds, football had returned to normality too, which meant that the FA's promise of a visit to Wembley for an England game had come to fruition. I was invited to be a guest at a match between England and Andorra. It proved an unforgettable day in ways I'd never anticipated. Sarah wasn't a football fan so I took two of my closest friends, Haydn and Ryan. It made me really happy to share some of my success with those who'd helped me along the way. Deep down too, I think, a part of me still hurt at the suggestion I'd ignored them when the quiz took off.

★

We travelled down on the train and, arriving at Wembley, were led into our own function room with a free bar and food, where we mingled with several other members of the twenty-three-strong Lionhearts squad. During the build-up to the match, there was an announcement over the PA system. I couldn't believe my eyes when the giant display screens around the ground flashed up images of each of the members, including me. It was *Boy's Own* dream stuff for me. How could I have ended up on a giant scoreboard at Wembley? It was insane.

It was while I was in the private box mixing with some of the other Lionhearts during half-time that I noticed a family. I recognised the little girl from the media. She had been the final person to be nominated for the Lionheart award. Her name was Daisy Briggs, and she was three years old. She had been born with spina bifida and hydrocephalus and was unlikely ever to be able to walk without a frame. She had seen Captain Tom completing his walking challenge the previous summer and had decided to do something similar. Daisy used her walking frame to walk 25 metres a day wearing a different colour of the rainbow and had raised an amazing £25,000 for NHS Charities Together.

I saw she was with her parents. I couldn't help looking at her dad – he looked vaguely familiar. Throughout the rest of the match, I was racking my brains trying to place him. After the game had finished and while finishing off our drinks, he came over to me.

'It's Jay, isn't it? I know you live in Lancashire now, but are you originally from London?'

'I am,' I nodded, my mind whizzing at a thousand miles an hour.

It's weird how the brain works. Before he could say another word, somehow I dug out a name from my distant past, from my days at Tamworth Manor school.

'Is your name Sean Briggs?'

'It is. We were mates at school.'

It was true. I'd not had a huge number of close friends at school, but he was one of them. We hadn't spoken to or seen each other since those distant days, more than a quarter of a century earlier.

We spoke briefly, mainly about Daisy and how proud we – but especially he – was of her. I showed him a photo of Jack. We were soon being separated; people had begun to leave the hospitality box and begin their journeys home. I wished Sean and Daisy and her mum, Rea, well and headed off with Haydn and Ryan.

They were gobsmacked when I told them I'd met an old school friend. They knew a fair bit about my past by now.

'Wasn't all bad then,' Haydn said, as we sat on the train.

It stopped me in my tracks a little. He was right. Too often in recent years I'd just seen my childhood as a dark time, a period that I'd survived rather than experienced as a normal kid. But there had been good times. I hadn't always been this unhappy nonentity of a boy I had pictured in my head. I had made friendships. I had, somehow, registered in people's lives.

Perhaps I needed to remind myself of that every now and again.

★

Eventually, I had a letter confirming that the investiture ceremony for my MBE would happen late in the year. The date was finally set for November 2021, at Windsor Castle.

I was told that I was allowed to bring a 'plus one', which was obviously going to be Sarah. The dress code was formal, so we both had to hit the shops in Manchester. I bought a new three-piece suit, while Sarah chose a lovely floral dress and fascinator. Sarah wasn't one to wear dresses often. But we both agreed – if you didn't dress up for this, then what on earth did you dress up for?

Sadly, by then the Duke of Edinburgh had passed away and The Queen had become increasingly frail. Alex had very good connections to the royal family, so had put out feelers to see who might be presenting me with the medal. At first, I was over the moon when he said it was Prince William. We were roughly the same age, and I was an admirer. But the nervousness soon set in. As the clock ticked down to the ceremony, I was just a nervous wreck.

We travelled down from Darwen to Windsor the day before and booked into the hotel that overlooks Windsor Castle and the famous Long Walk that leads up to it. We had a little stroll around the town during the afternoon and evening. It was quiet, but its connection to the royal family was obvious everywhere. It just added to our sense of excitement. And my nerves.

I slept fitfully that night. A couple of times I got up, drew back the curtains of our hotel room and looked up towards the unmistakeable Round Tower of Windsor Castle. The vast stone walls of the fortress were glowing against the inky black sky, illuminated by a colourful, festive light show. Every now and again I would see the silhouette of a soldier or a sentry walking through the grounds, picked out by the lights and magnified a hundred times against the wall.

There had been plenty of 'pinch me' moments in the past two years, but this felt a hundred times bigger too.

The next morning, I barely ate a mouthful of breakfast. It was as if someone had reached inside me and wrapped their hands tight around my stomach. It was butterflies on steroids.

There was a lot of media work to be done in advance of the ceremony the following morning. I spoke to our local station, BBC Radio Lancashire. We then got into our finery and drove up the Long Walk towards the entrance to the castle.

The security was like nothing I'd ever encountered. The underside of the car was checked with long mirrors; they opened up our boot and checked inside. We'd been asked to bring our passports as ID too, as well as up-to-date COVID tests. We'd done the tests a couple of days earlier. It had taken an age to get the results back. Today, it seemed to take just as long for the sentries and police officers to inspect our passports. We were so close to getting inside the castle walls, but even at that point I was half expecting one of the uniformed officers to politely escort me back down the Long Walk and send me on my way. *I'm afraid there's been a terrible mistake, Mr Flynn,* he would say. But it didn't happen. Instead, we were let through and invited to drive into a car park within the huge castle's battlements.

We were then ushered into a reception area, where we were greeted by the small army of equerries and courtiers who were running the investiture ceremonies that day.

It was a shame in many ways. Ordinarily, all the recipients are gathered together in the same place beforehand so that they can mingle and congratulate each other. But today we were ushered into the Great Hall to join a small group moving along in a well-drilled line. I could see the tall, slightly balding figure of Prince William in the distance ahead of me, deep in conversation with another recipient.

There were only one or two recipients ahead of me and I was soon at the front of the queue. My heart was racing, and I could just see Sarah. She was being ushered by a smartly uniformed courtier to the other side of the room, where she could have a good view of the proceedings. She looked fit to burst with excitement – and pride.

As I stood there, the usual imposter syndrome crept into my head. Why am I here? I don't deserve it. This is a mistake. But then

I heard my name called. 'Mr Johnny James Flynn. Host, Virtual Pub Quiz. For charitable service during Covid-19.'

I'd been briefed on the next bit. I was to step forward and stand alongside one of the castle's guards. I was then to follow his lead with military precision. Step forward three paces, stop, turn, step forward five paces, keeping my shoulder aligned with the guard at all times. I then gave the most awkward of bows before raising myself to face the tall figure that was now looming over me.

I'd gone over what to say a million times in my head, but had the wind taken out of my sails immediately.

'Jay, I am so honoured to meet you,' Prince William said in his familiar baritone voice. 'I have been looking forward to this and can't wait to find time to play one of your quizzes.'

My head was a mess. Had I heard that right? The future king of England had said that he was honoured to meet me! Surely it was the other way round?

It was then that the penny dropped. It wouldn't have surprised me if everyone in the chamber had heard it. The enormity of what was happening hit me.

I didn't have time to dwell on it.

We spoke for a few minutes. He said that quizzes were one of the great British pastimes and he'd been amazed at how many people had played along with me each Thursday. I said I owed my success to a lot of people and was going to dedicate the award to them. The rest of the conversation was a blur. Before I knew it, my time was over. I stepped back, bowed and turned to walk to Sarah, who had a beaming smile on her face. We were ushered into another huge anteroom, lined with all sorts of artefacts and treasures from the royal household. While I did some press, Sarah walked around the room guided by a courtier who explained the assorted exhibits to her.

We then stepped outside into the morning air and had our photographs taken. They were the standard shots you see in the newspapers when the great and the good and the famous get their gongs.

Sarah and I leaned into each other while I held up the medal in its beautiful velvety case. I still couldn't quite compute the fact that this was me going through that well-rehearsed routine.

Because of COVID, the reception afterwards was minimal, which was fine by me. I wanted to drive back to Darwen. I was desperate to show the medal to Jack. I had also arranged a small get-together with friends in a local pub. It was the appropriate way to celebrate, back where this had all started and among the people who had supported me.

Jack gave me the biggest hug when I got through the door. He was impressed by the medal but had something more important on his mind.

'Can I take it to school to show my friends?' he said.

'Of course,' I said, already panicking in case it got lost or damaged.

We put Jack to bed then headed off to the pub, leaving Sarah's mum to look after him. On the way there, a million thoughts passed through my mind, as usual.

The photos of me receiving the MBE had already made the local news. BBC Radio Lancashire had run their interview with me and apparently there had been a small item on the BBC TV news that night. As we walked through town, one lady raised her thumbs at me and shouted, 'Done us proud, Jay.' We passed a guy who I'd known vaguely from The Greenfield. 'Thought you'd be having dinner with royalty tonight,' he joked, giving me a pat on the back as he went by.

There were a couple of ways we could have walked, but at a junction on our route I stopped, an idea forming.

'Sarah, let's go the long way.'

'Why?' she said.

'You'll see.'

We did a small detour and soon saw a familiar building looming into view.

The Crown had reopened again by now. It looked dead, barely a soul in there. I looked inside and saw little had changed. It had had a lick of paint but nothing beyond that.

'That was a good decision,' Sarah said, shaking her head knowingly.

'Yep. That's why I wanted to come past,' I said.

We pressed on, heading towards the other pub, where our friends were all waiting for us.

'I've come up with a lot of wrong answers in my time,' I said. 'But thank God I got that one right.' It felt like the biggest understatement of my life.

★

A week after our visit to Windsor Castle I was back down south, sitting on the bench on the Embankment, lost in my thoughts after performing the unveiling of the plaque an hour or so earlier. The sun had disappeared and the temperature had dropped, adding a bite to the light breeze coming off the Thames. I always enjoyed coming back to London. It was my home town. It was in my blood. I missed its buzz, I missed its craziness, its unpredictability. As if to remind me of its magic, an eccentric-looking character in dreadlocks and a high-vis yellow jacket wobbled past on a rickety old bicycle, singing happily to himself. It shook loose a memory, from a morning in the run-up to my first Christmas sleeping rough. Back in December 2007.

I'd woken up to a surprise. Someone had left a twenty-pound note inside the top of my sleeping bag. But they'd left something else as well. It was resting against the bench. An old bicycle, complete with a simple note. *For you.*

I pocketed the money, grateful for the donation. But I wasn't sure what I was going to do with the other gift. I inspected the bike. It had certainly seen better days. Its paint was flaked and there was rust on the handlebars, but it was functioning – just. It was early and the streets were all but deserted, so I decided to give the bike a test drive. *Why not?* I figured. I loaded up my rucksack, slung it over my shoulder, boarded the bike and pushed off. I couldn't recall the last time I'd cycled. I might have been ten years old. It took me a while to steady myself – the weight of my rucksack had thrown off my equilibrium and, for a moment or two, I zigzagged wildly along the pavement. But I was soon moving along nicely and steered the bike onto the empty road. It was good to feel the breeze in my hair and to travel along the river in the early-morning light. As I got the knack of it, I speeded up a little, pedalling harder. My imagination kicked in as usual and I was soon picturing myself cycling through the suburbs of the city and out into the countryside, freewheeling my way through the English landscape without a care in the world.

I turned off the road and cycled into the beautiful little park that runs alongside the Embankment and the river, weaving my way on the path through the greenery. Aside from a single jogger, the park was empty. I felt like I had London to myself, as if I was in one of those post-apocalyptic movies where I was the last man on Earth. I was having a ball. My adrenaline levels had obviously risen because at one point I began to wonder whether this was an omen. A sign of things to come. Maybe the bike was the future? I'd cycle the length and breadth of the UK on it. Maybe even take it onto the Continent. The notion didn't last long.

I came out of the park and re-entered the main road. I got as far as Blackfriars Bridge, where the Embankment footpath came to an end. By now, the traffic had begun to build and I felt the force of a couple of giant articulated lorries whoosh past me. As I swerved to avoid a pothole, I also crossed paths with a van driver. He gave me a blast of his horn and a single-fingered salute. I snapped back to reality. And an attack of common sense. What was I thinking?

Temperatures had been dropping the past couple of days and a cold snap was predicted. The previous night I'd told myself that I needed to find some real warmth that day, preferably on a Tube or a bus. I wasn't going to take a bike down into the Underground with me. It was too cumbersome. It would be too much trouble wheeling it around. And where would I keep it safely? I wasn't going to fork out on an expensive padlock.

On the road leading up off the Embankment on to Blackfriars Bridge I spotted a bike rack, half full. I crossed the road and wheeled the bike up there, placing it carefully in a spare space. I'd kept the note the person had left me and placed it back in the basket. *For you.* I hoped someone else would have a better use for it.

I returned to my routine and disappeared down into Blackfriars Tube station, in search of a Travelcard. For a moment I felt a little guilty. Ungrateful. But I knew that wasn't the right attitude. Sometimes, gifts are for the moment. The bike had given me one, a few fleeting minutes of escapism. I'd enjoyed it and I was grateful for that. It was time for someone else to have their moment now.

★

I'd got so lost in the memory that I'd lost track of the time. I heard the distinctive bongs of Big Ben and saw that I needed to get moving. My train back to Darwen would be leaving within the hour. Sarah and Jack would be expecting me back for supper.

I got up and took another look at the plaque, glinting in the dull wintry light. I couldn't help laughing to myself. The reason I'd been asked to unveil the little memorial was that it was actually dedicated to me. It had been the idea of a group of my closest Patreon support- ers – the Jayders, as they were affectionately known. Without me knowing, they'd approached Westminster City Council and, once they'd got it approved, paid for the plaque and its fixing themselves. Only then had they sprung the surprise on me. When they'd asked me to come down to London to unveil it, I couldn't really have said no.

The plaque read:

> *Number 3, Riverside View. This bench*
> *was home to Jay Flynn from Jay's Virtual Pub Quiz.*
> *He proves you are not alone and there is always hope.*

Even in my most fanciful, far-fetched flights of imagination, I would never have come up with such a story. But it had happened. It was true. The evidence was staring me in the face. My time on this bench had been marked for posterity, complete with a message that, with luck, would resonate long after I'd gone.

I gave the plaque a final little rub with my sleeve and smiled.

At times, sleeping here on the bench in all weathers, I had felt utterly alone. That my life was immaterial. That no one would miss me if I wasn't there. And that I truly didn't have any hope. Of course, I'd been wrong. The person who had left me the twenty-pound note and the bike that cold Christmas was just one example. Plenty of other people proved it too, along the way. And had continued to do so in the years since I'd left my riverside refuge.

I was gathering my stuff ready to head home when that quote came back to me again. *We each lead two lives, the one we learn with and the one we live after that.*

As I'd processed its meaning earlier, I'd felt proud of the way that, without knowing it, I'd put the lessons of my first life to good use. Not just in the life I'd built with Sarah and Jack, but also, I hoped, in the way I'd dealt with the unexpected hand fate had dealt me back in March 2020.

I hadn't anticipated any of it, of course. I'd just been acting on a hunch. I'd taken a bold guess. That somebody, somewhere, might get some solace, some company and maybe even some entertainment if I asked fifty questions on a Thursday night.

I smiled again. The questions now forming in my head weren't ones I'd asked myself before. In all the interviews I'd done, no journalist had posed them either.

So what was the greatest lesson I learned from the whole experience? What, if anything, had it proved? The answer came to me immediately. It was staring me in the face – literally – engraved on that plaque. I nodded to myself. Yes, that said it all really.

We aren't alone. And there is always hope.

ACKNOWLEDGEMENTS

So where do you start when it comes to this bit – who to thank first, in which order, is one more valuable than the other? Well, in my mind, no, everyone here is equally deserving of thanks.

So I'm going to start with my mum. The reason that I am even in this world. Forty-one years has been at times hard and challenging for us both. For eleven years, you had the burden of not knowing if I was even OK. But now the relationship we have is more solid than it has ever been. The process of writing this book has been so hard, but you have supported me every step of the way. You have helped me pick through some of my more befuddled memories while trying to work through your own befuddled memories. But I am grateful to have you in my life now and you are a wonderful grandma to Jack. All I can really do is say thank you.

And Conor, in your own unique way, thank you for still managing to be that little brother, even though you very much aren't that any more!

Garry, I would wager there have been times during this that you have regretted replying to our initial messages! I know it's been hard trying to work your way through my at times incoherent ramblings, but if the writing game goes wrong, you have a solid career in therapy there, ready to go if you need it!

To my ragtag bag of misfit friends, I'm not going to name each and every one of you, so if you read this and think 'where is my name?', then know that I am grateful for our friendships. But I do want to thank a few personally, starting with Ryan. Mate, we might have sold a lot more cars were it not for our weekly Wednesdays writing that night's quiz in the office when all the bosses had gone home! Haydn, you and Sharon are both incredibly supportive. If everyone were as laid back as you at times, the world would be a much better place. Sil (sorry Andrew!) and Scott, you two have been there for my big moments. Friends from the moment I arrived in Wigan, with me when I met Sarah and gave her the seal of approval, by my side when we got married, there when Jack came into the world. The brilliant thing with our friendship is that you are both there, no matter what. Even if I don't reply, or answer your call, we know we are a solid part of each other's lives and I thank you and Kayleigh and Rachel for your support. And the final two to mention: Roy, not much I can say about you really, because you'll just moan about it. Thank you for being you, pal. Paige, in a short space of time we have shared so many different things together. We have memories and so many inside jokes it's unreal. I might mock you at times, but you are a talented graphic designer and I'm grateful to have you in my life.

Gill, thank you for being an incredible mother-in-law. At the time Sarah came into my life, I was lost, and you welcomed me into the family and have been an incredible source of support and comfort. You do so much to help everyone, and especially Sarah and me – we are so incredibly grateful. I'm struggling to find the actual words to use, but I think you know without me saying anything. The fact that we are the two sensible and sane ones in the family really is saying something.

Alex, these last few years wouldn't have been possible without you. You have a unique ability to achieve the impossible and never get worked up or stressed out about anything. It's been humbling, having you in my corner, helping me fight some of those demons that would creep up, and being my biggest supporter. The majority of the things that happened would never have been achieved without your hard work and relentless tenacity, and for that I will be forever grateful.

Bek, my Haribo- and meal-deal-sharing friend. When Alex and I knew that things were getting out of control and we needed someone to take the weight off us, there was never ever a second option. It was you or nothing. Because you are so incredibly talented at what you do. But it goes way beyond the work you do, it's your friendship, it's your support. I always said I look upon you as my little sister, and I am so proud of the things you have achieved, and continue to achieve. You are always in my corner, always fighting for me, keeping me sane, keeping me thinking positively. Everyone needs a Bek in their life!

Zoe and the whole team at Radio 2. What started as a simple throwaway at the end of the interview has become a staple of the week for so many people. Such a talented group of people and I'm honoured to say that I play a small part in the incredible show.

Sarah. So where the hell do we start here? Over ten years and counting. Despite all your conditions, and everything you go through, you still function and take every little thing in your stride. These last few years have been challenging, but we work it all out and get through it. When we first met, we both knew straight away this was it – we'd found the missing puzzle piece. You, me and our tiny little terror can achieve anything we want to do – well, apart from getting you to meet Westlife, but I'm trying! You are my number one supporter and, along with Jack, you make the world a brighter place. Thank you, for being you.

And so to the final few people. To everyone at Hodder, thank you so much, guys, for putting your faith in me to produce the words that are contained in these pages. I'm a pain at times, I don't understand a lot of how this whole book process works, but you are all so patient, and incredibly talented.

Lesley, my agent, the same as the team at Hodder: your professionalism and honesty when faced with me asking stupid questions and at times being a pain is second-to-none in my opinion. I am so grateful to have you in my corner, helping guide me through this unknown world.

The Patreons. Thank you, because without your support, none of this would have been possible as I'd have been back in the motor trade. I'm honoured to have met a few of you, formed friendships, attended your weddings and been a part of your lives, so thank you so much for being a part of this story.

And finally, to you, the reader. This has been such an incredibly hard thing to do. To open up Pandora's box and lay myself bare for the world to read. There are some topics covered in here that won't be easy for some of you. But if writing this book has helped just one person to seek help or change their life, then I'll be very happy.

Darwen, Lancashire 2023

ABOUT THE AUTHOR

Jay Flynn is 'the nation's quizmaster' through his online quiz and with his slot on Zoe Ball's Radio 2 show. He lives in Lancashire with his wife Sarah, an NHS administrator, and their young son. He's previously published two quiz books. He writes all his own quiz questions.